Publication #16 in the "On Target"
series of Outdoor Sports Publications
from Target Communications
Outdoor Books

1st Printing: 4/04
2nd Printing: 7/07
3rd ng: 7/11
4th ng: 4/14
g: 2/17

CORE ARCHERY

Shooting with Proper Back Tension

- - -

Using Mental Mastery to Build Winning Form
Step-by-Step

by Larry Wise

Library of Congress Control Number: 2003117071

TARGET COMMUNICATIONS OUTDOOR BOOKS
10459 N. Wauwatosa Rd.
Mequon, WI 53097
www.targetcommbooks.com
P: 1-262-242-3530   F: 1-262-518-0341

ISBN: 0-913305-18-9

DEDICATION

On behalf of the thousands of archers who have benefited from his words of wisdom, his profound insights into shooting and his infectious positive attitude, I dedicate this book to

Bud Fowkes.

He is an inspiration to all who know him. He has been and continues to be my mentor and fellow coach, but what I value most is his friendship. Thank you, Bud.

THANKS TO THE FOLLOWING:

Fred Warner . . . for first asking, "How do we define Back Tension?"

Dr. Guy Schenker, D.C. . . . who helped me accurately define it.

Bud Fowkes . . . for teaching me how to "see" good form.

Ben Summers . . . for helping on the cover art.

Susie Thorn . . . for helping on the cover art.

Mark Martin . . . for modeling for the cover and other photos.

Bill Esborn . . . for exchanging ideas about form and the mental game.

Todd Wise . . . for all his technical assistance and his patience for his father.

Diana . . . for all her support for my crazy archery projects.

Glenn Helgeland . . . for his outstanding questions, suggestions and publishing abilities.

TABLE of CONTENTS

A unique ninth chapter, utilizing 44 photos of one shot to show
you the steps of a good archery shot as that shot is being built.
The photos are on 44 consecutive right hand pages and spring to
life as you thumb rapidly through them. Study the flow from one
image to the next to identify how each of the 12 form-steps leads
into the next. Made from a 30-second video of the author making
one well-executed shot.

What is Core Archery?

Core Archery is a complete system of archery shooting form. It is presented in this book as the sequence of proper mental and physical actions required to launch an arrow to the target center. What is significant about this system over others is that it is complete and repeatable. It consists only of the necessary and sufficient actions needed and has been validated by numerous archers, including myself, in past and present years.

You've seen Core Archery in action in others or even experienced it yourself but couldn't explain it or find it again when you lost it. This book gives you the insight into good archery form that will allow you to find the form you've lost or to gain it for the first time. Most important, when you learn Core Archery you'll be able to repeat your form.

Why is Core Archery about BACK TENSION?

Several months ago a group of men came to me for coaching. They wanted to improve their form to compete more on the 3-D tour, so they came for a Friday night and Saturday session. As our involvement in Core Archery progressed, one of the men asked the very insightful question, "Why do you teach archery by emphasizing back tension?"

This archer really wanted to know if I knew what I was talking about! He wanted to know if I was just making this up as a way to promote my archery schools or if I had a good, well thought out reason. He deserved an answer because he traveled two hundred miles and was paying for my time, so I gave him, and I give to you, this response.

I teach back tension because, of all the different ways to release an arrow, **controlling the release by utilizing your back muscles is the most consistent.** If you're not using your rhomboid muscles, then you have to substitute with arm muscles, which are more difficult to control and, therefore, less likely to repeat a precise motion. Back tension is all about repetition with a few short back muscles, and my years of shooting and winning have proven to me that it's better than any other method.

As Bud Fowkes has said -- actually preached -- for years, archery is a simple two-step sport:

Step 1:   Learn to shoot a ten.

Step 2:   Repeat step one!

You may find this humorous at first, but let's look at it closely. You can learn to shoot a ten in many different ways, but when you get to step two you falter because the way you learned to shoot is not repeatable. At least it's not repeatable with a high enough frequency to satisfy your desire to score well. With that in mind, read on and learn to build repeatable form, learn to build Core Archery.

Why is Core Archery about using your skeletal structure properly?

Your form will repeat if you are using your body properly. That is, if you are using your core -- your spine -- correctly. Following that, by efficiently positioning the rest of your skeleton around it, you will be able to build a form that repeats. Also, you will resist fatigue far better than those who fail to use their skeleton efficiently.

Core Archery, therefore, is a systematic set of archery form steps built around the proper use of your skeleton. Throughout each form step the governing theme is to maximize skeleton while minimizing muscle. **If you do this, your form will be energy efficient, fatigue resistant and highly repeatable.**

As you read about each step of Core Archery form, you will learn how it links to the next step and how all of the steps relate to the final shooting objective of "back tension execution". These links are what makes the Core Archery form system easy to evaluate and repair. Compared to what you're doing now, linked steps keep your form nearer peak performance.

Why is Core Archery about mental skills?

When your form is physically complete and practiced so it operates through the subconscious mind, you must develop good mental skills to help you score high under all conditions. Good mental control enables you to relax when others are tense, and that takes you to STEP 2 while others are wrestling with STEP 1.

Keep these things in mind as you read Core Archery, and good luck becoming a STEP 2 archer.

CHAPTER ONE

YOUR SHOOTING OBJECTIVE

WHY DO YOU NEED A SHOOTING OBJECTIVE?

When you get in your car, start it and drive down your driveway or street, you usually have a destination in mind. It's not often we just drive around without going "somewhere". Few contractors I know build houses or other buildings without a plan or blueprint. For most archers, however, the only objective **(1)** when they nock an arrow is to shoot it into the ten-ring or "x".

I want the arrow to hit the "x", too, but to those who want to excel, archery is more than arrows hitting targets. Taking archery seriously means that you must organize what your body is doing prior to releasing the arrow. **At the highest performance level, archery is all about how you control your body and mind while executing a sequence of steps known as FORM.**

To be successful in anything, you must have an appropriate and specific objective. In archery, this objective must focus on how you direct your body actions. **"How will I use my body to shoot an arrow, and what is my concluding, objective step?"** is the question you must answer about yourself.

Do you have an objective? Or do you, like so many other archers, just follow a loosely organized set of steps until the arrow

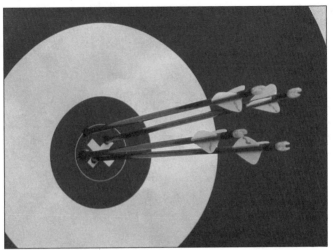

• 1: 3-D, field and target archery require repeatable form. The groups that result make high scores. Repeatable form for bowhunting greatly increases your chances of success.

is released and immediately grab your binoculars to see if you hit the ten-ring?

Then the questions come streaming at you. If you didn't hit the middle, did you have bad form? If you believe that you had good form, how do you know? By what standard are you measuring your form steps? What objective in your form are you not meeting when you miss?

If you can't answer these questions, ask the following two: Will having a shooting objective improve my performance? What shooting objective will get me the best results? These are valid questions you must be able to answer if you plan to build a shooting form that will provide consistent, long-term results.

Let me repeat:

You must have the correct shooting objective if you want consistent, long-term results!

THE SHOOTING OBJECTIVE

The shooting objective I teach in Core Archery is:

Shoot each arrow using the appropriately timed execution of back tension.

It's so simple to state, but it requires self-discipline to learn and apply. There are easier ways to shoot arrows but none more effective or more enduring. Using back tension to conclude an archery shot is a must if you want to succeed in tournament archery or when bowhunting. Yes, bowhunting, because often you get only one chance in hunting, and you had better have reliable form for that one shot or you'll miss, or worse yet, get a non-vital hit.

The advantage of this objective is the fact that you can use it to measure every step of your form. Every step of Core Archery form relates directly to the final objective of back tension. Each form step can be evaluated for its effectiveness and its place in the form

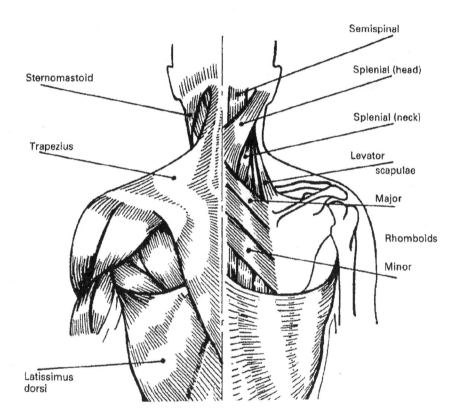

• 2: The important muscles of the back, as far as archery is concerned, are the rhomboids and levator scapulae. The trapezius is next in importance because it links the entire shoulder into a unit.

Archery Anatomy by Ray Axford. Subhead: An Introduction to Techniques for Improved Performances. Used by permission of Souvenir Press, copyright 1995.

sequence because, "In archery you must not only do the right things, you must do them at the right time." . . . Bud Fowkes, 1972 United States Olympic Archery Coach.

In other words, archery is not about bows and arrows, it's about you and your ability to control your body consistently to achieve a desired outcome. In Core Archery, you focus on body position and proper use of your body's core, your SKELETON.

DEFINING BACK TENSION

Now that you know what your objective should be, you must learn to acquire it. To do that, you first need definitions to the two key terms – "back tension" and "full draw position". Understanding how these apply to your shooting form is critical to your success in implementing back tension.

BACK TENSION is the contraction of the dominant or drawing-side rhomboid muscles, aided by the levator scapulae muscle, which causes a micro sliding-rotation of the scapula toward the spine.

Illustration 2 shows the location of these muscles and how the scapula is moved when they are contracted. The movement is small, but that's why it's easier to control and more consistent. Working these small muscles allows you to relax longer and more - difficult-to-control arm muscles that can be far less consistent to operate.

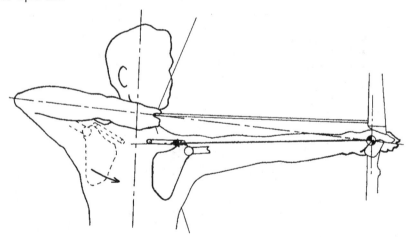

• 3: Contracting your draw side rhomboid muscles will cause your scapula to slide and rotate toward your spine.

While the rhomboids and levator scapulae muscles are contracting, the trapezius muscle **(2)** also contracts, locking the shoulder unit with the scapula, keeping them both close to the rib cage, and moving the draw-arm and hand enough to cause a release aid or a draw check device to activate.

There it is. That's the true objective of good form every time you nock an arrow. Every piece of your form must be geared to setting up the proper execution of back tension. If not, then whatever you're doing is wasting energy or working against your performance. Worse, it can cause damage to your body, for which you'll pay later.

As you read the next few chapters on building your form, keep this definition in mind. This definition is the main difference between the Core Archery system and other systems. Without the correct objective, other systems fall far short in their effectiveness. They also fall short in their ability to sustain your level of success over long periods of time. And when you do have those periods of struggle, you can work yourself out of them sooner because you know how all of your form steps must fit together to achieve the specific outcome of properly timed back tension. You always have that standard of comparison to measure against.

BACK AND SHOULDER MUSCLES

Now, do you need to know these muscle names and locations? I think so; knowing more about your objective can help you better

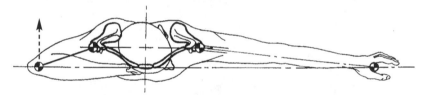

• 4: When the rhomboids, levator scapulae and trapezius muscles are contracted, they cause the upper arm and elbow to rotate about the shoulder joint, as shown.

• 5: Notice that in proper full-draw position the drawing forearm is in line with the arrow, thus allowing the "holding" to be fully transferred into the back muscles.

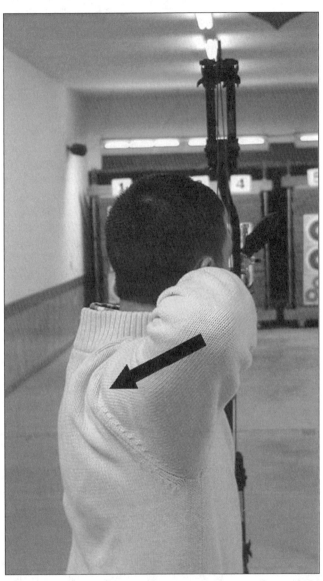

• 6: Once again, when the rhomboids, levator scapulae and trapezius muscles are shortened during contraction they will cause the upper arm and elbow to rotate about the shoulder joint. The anatomy of the shoulder allows the upper arm to rotate naturally about the shoulder joint in a plane tilted about thirty-degrees from horizontal as shown here. Learning to establish this rotational force without other unnecessary muscle tension gives you the ability to aim steady while executing the release with highest level of finesse and accuracy. You will work smarter rather than harder! Proper setup and execution of the back tension process allows the release hand to follow-through directly away from behind the arrow.

plan how you can achieve it. Learning where these muscles are located, what they feel like when you contract them and how to position your body will enable you to get the most out of them.

Figure 2 shows the major and minor rhomboids along with the levator scapulae muscle. Contracting these muscles will rotate the scapula (shoulder blade) toward the spine **(3)**. Because the scapula is connected to the shoulder, moving the scapula toward the spine causes the shoulder unit to pivot in the horizontal plane. The upper arm follows this pivot motion and the elbow is also pulled backward **(5)** in the horizontal plane, perpendicular to the shooting direction. The draw-arm and hand follow the shoulder, and this movement can efficiently and effectively be used to execute the release of the arrow.

Figure 2 also shows the trapezius and how it performs its function of keeping the shoulder blade close to the rib cage while linking the shoulder unit to the scapula. This link, when used properly, enables the short rhomboids to initiate a releasing sequence much more accurately and efficiently than longer and bigger muscles can.

DEFINING FULL DRAW POSITION

Question: What happens immediately before you execute back tension?

Answer: You must reach full draw position. Right?

Yes. So how far do you draw your bow to make this happen? That depends on you and how you fulfill the following definition.

FULL DRAW POSITION is that position to which you draw the bowstring, using proper body alignment, in order to place your scapula in the most effective position for executing back tension.

As mentioned earlier, good archery is about maintaining proper body position throughout each step of the shooting act. The next-to-last step in this act is getting the scapula into position near -- but not as close as it can get – to the spine. The scapula must be able to move a small amount when you contract your rhomboids, otherwise this contraction will be ineffective and your arms will still have to perform the shot execution.

Full-draw-position must be established according to illustrations 4, 5 and 6. In these illustrations you can see that the drawing forearm and elbow are (top view) in line with the arrow. This position allows the holding effort to be fully transferred into the back muscles while positioning the scapula near the spine. It's critical that your bow fits your position.

Your full draw position can have various secondary reference points on your face and neck that you can use to increase consistency in reaching full draw. However, primary attention should be placed on the position of the drawing-side scapula and shoulder unit. Most archers I know mis-focus on the touch point on their face or jaw and never consider the placement of their scapula. In other words, they focus on getting anchored and not on executing back tension. Without proper focus, they do not get the most consistent results.

• 7: Any individual or group can check eye dominance by first extending their arms to full length. Then, while looking at your face, they bring their arms and hands together, forming a small hole between their hands. This hole will form around their dominant eye.

• 8: The student on the left has closed his hands to a small hole showing that he has right-eye dominance. The other student, much to his surprise, has left-eye dominance, which told him to change his form for shooting basketball.

EYE DOMINANCE

Have you checked your eye dominance? If not, you should, so you can build your form on your most effective shooting side. Aiming with your non-dominant eye will necessitate closing your dominant eye. That can create unwanted tension in your face, neck and shoulders.

Here's a simple test you can do by yourself. **(7 & 8)** Stand and point your index finger at a small object, like a doorknob, about fifteen feet away. Now close your right eye. Does your fingertip move to the right? If so, your right eye was controlling your vision focus and is your dominant eye.

Now repeat the process but close your left eye. If your fingertip moves to the left, your left eye is dominant.

Now comes the tough part. You must shoot archery by drawing your bow with your dominant side. Doing this enables you to aim with your dominant eye. Few archers have been able to master aiming with their non-dominant eye. My recommendation is to aim with your dominant eye and maximize your chances of success.

WHY FORM STEPS?

Once you accept properly executed back tension as your objective, you also must realize that there must be a best way to reach it. **This best way consists of form steps which you must learn and practice.**

Organizing these steps is essential.

These steps must be done in a precise order and with precise movements to maximize the results. They also must take into account the differences among body shapes and sizes. Keep that in mind as you read the following chapters outlining the steps of good model form.

CHAPTER TWO
STAND

1. STANCE

Where do you begin when you want to build something? Of course, you begin with the foundation. In archery form, foundation means your stance. For some that's in a wheelchair, for others it's leaning against a stool or stand of some kind. For most, however, your stance is on two feet planted firmly on the ground.

Because we have defined a "shot-objective", your stance must permit you to achieve that objective consistently. Placing your feet on the ground can be done in a variety of ways. That begs the question "What's the best way for me?" Well, there's a method to check what's the best for you, and if you use it regularly you always will have your best stance.

EVEN/SQUARE STANCE

Lower body stability is what you want from your stance; using some reference lines on the floor can help you get it. Place an arrow or piece of tape on the floor so it is pointed directly at the target. Now stand with your toes touching the reference line to form an even or square stance. **(9)**

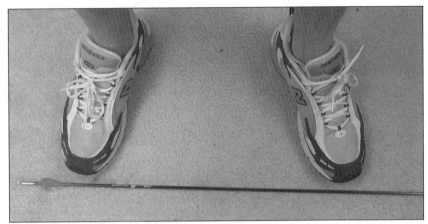

• 9: *Standing with both toes on a line to the target creates a square stance.*

A square stance places your body at right angles to the target and prepares you for raising the bow. Of course, you must turn your head, and only your head, 70 or 80 degrees to see the target. In this position you should be able to raise the bow, draw and aim at the target and complete the shot effectively without further shuffling of your feet.

Your feet should be spread apart to hip or shoulder width for maximum stability. Spreading too far will put undue pressure on your lower back and lead to fatigue. A narrow stance will not give you the needed stability for prolonged aiming success; you will sway. Swaying is not conducive to precise aiming.

OPEN STANCE

• 10: *An open stance has the target-side foot moved several inches back from the line to the target.*

Two other options are available for stance rotation relative to the target. The most common of these is the open stance that is attained by rotating your body-front several degrees so it somewhat faces the target. **(10)** Sliding your target-side foot a few inches away from the reference line on the floor creates the open stance.

With the front of your body now open to the target, your bow shoulder is rotated a few more degrees out of line with the arrow **(12a)**. It's difficult to create a perfect line with your drawing arm, arrow and bow arm because the string must have ample space to move forward behind the arrow. We deal with this situation the best way we can by keeping our draw-side shoulder rotated just a few degrees out of line. An open stance seems to do that for most archers.

CLOSED STANCE

• *11: Moving your target-side foot to the target line and your other foot away will make a closed stance.*

From an even stance, slide your rear foot several inches away from the reference line. This turns the front of your body slightly away from the target. Although this stance is not used by very many archers, some have found it to be best suited to their bodies. Hip anatomy and leg structure will lead you to try the closed stance. **(11)**

TESTING YOUR STANCE

What stance is right for you? That's the question you need to ask and answer regularly. Testing it frequently is important, since your form is constantly evolving. Consider that you're always getting older and changing bows from time to time and adjusting to the new set-up. Such changes can be subtle and take place over a long period of time, but they are always happening.

A simple test conducted at full draw can yield the answers you need about your stance. This test is used to determine your natural body drift while you're aiming. Once you know this drift tendency, you can adjust your stance to prevent it.

Start the test by assuming your chosen stance. Nock an arrow, raise your bow, draw and begin aiming at the target center. Now close your eyes and do your best to maintain position for eight seconds. Open your eyes and note the position of your sight. You've probably drifted down, but that's not important. Have you drifted left or right? That is the real question. Retest four or five times to be sure of your natural tendency.

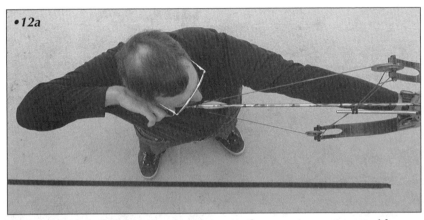

If you drift left during your closed-eye testing, reset your target-side foot closer to the line to make your stance slightly more toward square.

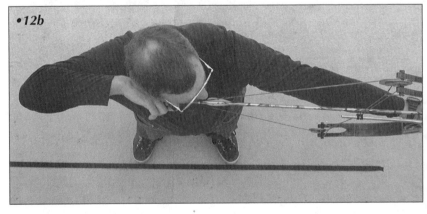

To compensate for a natural left drift, move your target-side foot two inches closer to a closed stance or move your target-side foot left two inches (**12a & b**). Repeat the closed eye test, noting positive or negative change and make small adjustments accordingly. Continue this testing for several practice sessions until you are sure of your stance.

Moving your target-side foot slightly toward the direct line to the target can eliminate a natural left drift. Retest with closed eyes for several practices to be sure of your new stance. After that, check your stance every other week or when using a new bow or changing draw weight or draw length. There's no need to fight your natural drift while aiming, so correct for it by altering your stance.

RELATION TO SHOOTING OBJECTIVE

Establishing a solid foundation is essential for a stable upper torso. If your upper body is wobbly and insecure, you will have little chance of repeating shot execution no matter how good you are at executing back tension. Paying close attention to how you set your stance and then maintaining that stance throughout the remainder of your shot sequence is essential to maximum success. If you set your stance correctly at the beginning, you won't have to change it later.

2. NOCK

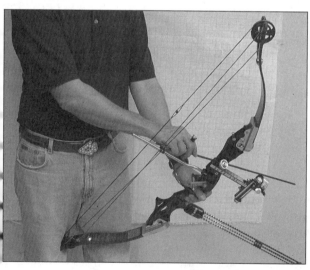

• 13: Keep your arms extended and relaxed while nocking your arrow.

Nocking an arrow on the string follows setting your stance. It sounds rather simple and not directly related to your shooting objective, but let's take a closer look at what a serious archer needs.

Taking a position on a shooting line or at a shooting stake defines a vertical plane **(13)** in which you plan to launch your arrow. This plane can be rather restrictive, as in the case of indoor shooting lanes where tilting your bow out of this plane may put it in someone else's lane. Learn from the beginning to keep your bow vertical or near vertical while nocking each arrow.

Bow and body movement should be kept to an absolute minimum to avoid wasting time and energy. Some tournaments require sixty to a hundred arrows, so wasting a little energy to nock each one adds up to a lot by the end of a scoring round. Economy of movement promotes staying in tune with your target line, which you established while setting your stance.

Your goal is a smooth drawing of arrow from quiver and snapping it onto the string. Your bow should be held still, in a low position but near vertical. This position should allow your arms to be relatively relaxed and your posture upright, so your next form step can be completed as efficiently as possible.

Setting and maintaining erect posture is of critical importance to archery form. Slumping or bending during any phase of your form sequence cannot and should not be tolerated. You can relax your arms between shots by allowing them to be extended while nocking an arrow, but don't give up good posture.

RELATION TO SHOOTING OBJECTIVE

Maintaining correct upper body position is extremely helpful in maintaining connection to your target line. As you initiate back tension, you need good posture and correct line. If you have maintained that during the nocking of your arrow, chances are better for having it at the end of your shot. Learn to nock your arrow with minimum movement, good vertical posture and minimal energy output.

3. BOWHAND POSITION

My mentor/coach, Bud Fowkes, has always stressed that the shot "begins and ends with bowhand position". He's right! Your bowhand is the first body part to touch the bow, even before the arrow is nocked, and it's the last body part to touch it as the arrow crosses the arrow rest. You must get it right from the very beginning so your shot has the best chance for success.

As you nock an arrow, your bowhand is already holding the bow handle in some fashion. (I hold mine loosely with my bow arm extended. While holding it loosely, I hook my release aid to the bowstring or, if I'm shooting with my fingers, I hold the string loosely with my release fingers.) At this point, you must set your bowhand position for the remainder of the shot sequence.

WHICH HAND PART TO USE

Examining your bowhand can provide you with some good strategy for hand placement. The outstanding visible mark on your palm is the lifeline or palmar crease **(14)**. Using that line as a reference, you can position your hand on the bow handle in different positions to note the feel.

The web of skin between your thumb and index finger is designed to collapse when pressure is applied to it and should be centered on the bow grip area. On my hand, that places the lifeline to the left of the grip-center and the pressure point between the handle and hand to the thumb-side of my lifeline.

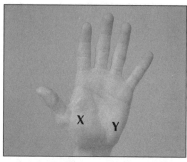

• 14: Make bow-grip contact with the thumb-side of your palm, marked X. In other words, touch the thenar eminence on the thumb-side of your palm to the bow grip. The hypothenar eminence (Y) should not touch the bow handle.

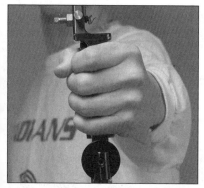 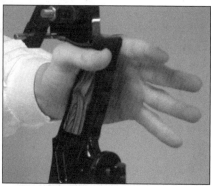

• 15a: Gripping the bow handle with your knuckles held vertically is not proper. Such a grip will put your forearm in front of the bowstring, and a stinging lesson is in store.

• 15b: Holding your fingers straight and stiff requires tightened muscles that promote torque in the grip.

When I'm coaching I look for contact between the student's hypothenar eminence **(Y, 14)** and the bow grip. This contact is a strong indication of improper hand position **(15)** in that the hand (little finger) is rotated too far downward. Extending the fingers on your bow hand **(15b)** also is improper and promotes handle torque.

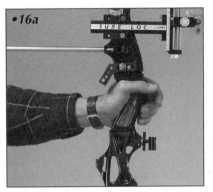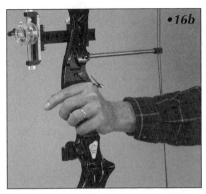

• 16 a & b: Proper hand position is achieved by keeping your knuckles at a 45-degree angle and your fingers relaxed.

The proper rotation of the hand will position the knuckles at about a 45-degree angle, with the vertical bow handle allowing contact between only the thenar eminence (ball of the thumb) and the bow grip area.

The wrist bones can resist the force-load of the bow most efficiently with a 45-degree rotation. By this, I mean that the force-loaded wrist will transfer the load directly to the large bone (radius) in your forearm, and from there through the upper arm bone (humerus), and onto the shoulder and back skeleton **(16a & b)**. If you fail to take advantage of this skeletal positioning; more muscle will be needed to carry the load and fatigue becomes a very real enemy of your shooting.

THE "STOP SIGN" TECHNIQUE

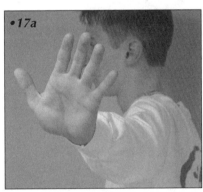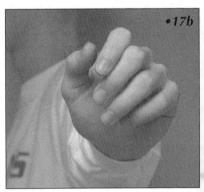

• 17a & b: To learn proper hand position, start with a "stop sign" formation, and then just relax your fingers. Don't change wrist position, just relax the fingers.

Stand

A neat method to teach this position involves making a "stop sign" with your bow hand **(17a & b)**. This technique has been around for years. It gives you a good look at the final position you'd like to attain when the bow is at full draw and aiming has begun. The trick is setting up for this position when you first place your hand in the grip area.

Once the stop sign is made, relax your fingers and thumb. Relax them completely! Don't drop your wrist, just relax your fingers. Your hand now is ready to resist the draw-force load of the bow. As you have experienced, gripping the handle with your fingers and/or thumb results in torque transfer to the bow handle. A lack of tension allows the bow handle and string to act more consistently. By keeping your hand and fingers relaxed, you can achieve repeatable bow-hand position.

BOW HANDLE PHYSICS

Maybe a little reminder of bow handle physics is in order here. What happens to the bow handle when the string is released? Good question, right? Most people say it thrusts forward toward the target.

Recall the principle of physics that states "for every action there is an equal and opposite reaction". It applies to the bow handle when the string is released **(18)**. As the small mass of the string moves a large distance toward the target, the much larger bow handle mass moves a small distance in the opposite direction, away from the target. That means it moves into your bowhand a very short distance for a very short time before it moves, in recoil, toward the target.

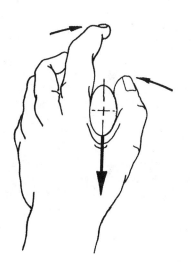

• **18: When the arrow is released, the string moves forward. The bow handle moves back into your hand before recoiling toward the target. A relaxed bowhand is most consistent during this bow movement.**

This movement is small, but it occurs as the arrow is crossing the arrow rest, and that makes it significant. A stiff or tight bow hand imparts torque to the bow handle at the instant the handle pushes into it. When the handle is torqued in any direction while the arrow is crossing the rest, the arrow is affected.

If your bowhand is tightened to some degree, the question becomes "Can you tighten your hand exactly to the same degree for every shot?" You know the answer, of course, and it's "No". You stand a much better chance of relaxing your hand to the same degree on every shot. This also eliminates the use of hand muscle, and that reduces the fatigue factor in your shooting form.

THE POINTING STRATEGY

Pointing at the target is another useful teaching technique for bowhand position. Point at the target with your bow hand index finger, then relax your fingers. Your bowhand is in nearly the same position as the stop sign technique, with your knuckles at about a 45-degree angle. Again, keeping it relaxed is the key and, yes, it's difficult to learn, but it works. It feels so natural after you learn it.

We humans are very controlling animals, thus it is natural for us to want to control the bow handle in an effort to make the arrow go where we want it. But by trying to control it we defeat our purpose; controlling promotes torque transfer and a variable launch pad. Bowhand consistency is like the butterfly analogy: "If you pursue the butterfly it is always just beyond your grasp, but, if you sit down quietly, it may come and light upon you."

SETTING THE BOW HAND

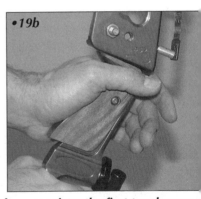

• 19a & b: To place your hand in the bow consistently, first touch your lifeline to the edge of the bow grip. Next, roll your hand up into the bow grip.

To get the bowhand into the position described, you need a plan. My plan consists of touching my bowhand lifeline **(19a)** to a point on the left edge of the bow grip area and then rolling my hand **(19b)** up and into the grip. Find and mark this reference point on your own grip and move your hand around until you find the point that gets you the best hand position.

Once you make this roll motion and set your hand, do not change it. Your hand must stay set in place during the raise and draw steps. After that, the only aspect that changes is the pressure with which the bow presses into your hand as you draw the bow. If you find that your hand is not in the right position during some phase of the shot, let the bow down and start over. Absolutely do not change hand position while raising, drawing or aiming your bow, as this action will introduce small torque loads into the set-up. There is only one time in your form sequence to set bow hand position, and that's after nocking your arrow and before setting release hand position. Start it right so the shot is finished right.

ELBOW ROTATION

Most archers I have coached need help setting bow hand position. Many also comment that their bowstring hits their arm occasionally. Of course, the two are related. Rotating your bowhand down (knuckles vertical) so your little finger is around the bow grip also rotates your forearm into a position where the bowstring will hit it.

• 20: Be sure to relax your fingers when setting your bow hand position.

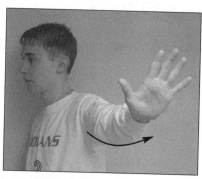

• 21: With your knuckles at a 45 degree angle, roll your forearm clockwise (for right-handers) out of the string path.

Proper knuckle rotation to 45 degrees **(20)** also creates the opportunity to rotate your elbow **(21)** 10 to 15 degrees outward (bow arm elbow clockwise) for right hand shooters. When you do this, your forearm will rotate out of the bowstring path and the bowstring won't strike it.

You'll need to practice this rotation as you set your bowhand. The two must be done in sequence until your subconscious automatically sets them in the proper position.

RELATIONSHIP TO YOUR SHOOTING OBJECTIVE

When your bowhand is set correctly, the draw force of the bow is transferred through the big bones of your arm and into your shoulder. From there it is transferred to your back skeleton. Your bowside shoulder and back must be stationary to provide aiming, but if the force is not transferred properly you cannot aim effectively. If you cannot aim effectively, you will not be able to apply your back tension technique effectively. Skeleton position and stability are critical to repeatability and, on the bow side, it begins with hand position.

• 22: After attaching your release aid, straighten your release wrist so your forearm muscles can be relaxed.

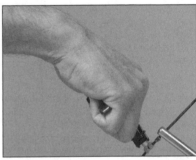

• 23: Bending your release wrist requires the contracting of forearm muscles. The result is unwanted muscle tension, which transfers up your arm and into your shoulder.

4. RELEASE HAND

After setting bow hand and elbow, turn your attention to your release hand. As mentioned, you've already attached your release to the string to maintain some tension on it while setting your bow hand. Now it's time to set the final position of your release hand.

Primary consideration must be given to your release-hand wrist position. Keeping your wrist straight **(22)** so hand and forearm are in the same plane enables you to relax your forearm muscles at full draw and make a more consistent release. In other words, only the two joints nearest your finger tips should be bent in order to grip your release aid or the string itself. From there, your hand should be straight through your wrist and forearm.

Bending your wrist and hand **(23)** requires forearm muscle contraction. With either the top or bottom forearm muscles contracted, your forearm tenses and transfers the tension to the upper arm for the duration of the shot. Once again, you've engaged in a high muscle-use technique that promotes fatigue and inconsistency.

Besides that, can you tense these muscles exactly the same for each shot? I doubt you can, so once again muscle relaxation is the skill most repeatable. Practicing this relaxation yields big results in minimizing left-right misses at the target.

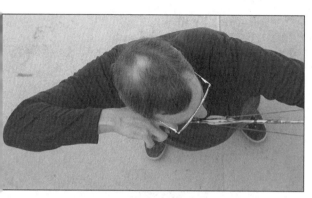

• 24: At full draw, a relaxed wrist and forearm will easily become an extension of the arrow.

As you begin to draw your bowstring, the pulling force will straighten a relaxed forearm and wrist **(24)**. If the wrist remains bent, then some forearm tension exists and too much muscle is being used. Your drawing arm should be used only as a connecting unit between your back/shoulder power center and the release hand. Relate this to the train cars between the engine and the caboose. Let the shorter back muscles control your archery and not the longer, harder to control arm muscles.

RELATION TO SHOOTING OBJECTIVE

Yes, some arm muscle use is necessary for drawing your bow, but by the time you get to full draw position these muscles must be relaxed and the shot control given over to the rhomboid muscle groups. A straight release wrist is your best chance for relaxing forearm and upper arm at full draw and maximizing consistency.

5. HEAD AND SHOULDER POSITION

Good posture is essential throughout every phase of your form sequence. If you give in to slouching, then you have to recreate good posture somewhere in your sequence. Recreating takes more energy and opens the door for the fatigue monster. Keep the erect posture you established when you set your stance.

That said, you now have to make a final setting of your head and shoulder position. When you are already erect, with shoulders level **(25a & b)** and not slumped forward, your upright head should be looking straight along the shooting line in front of you. As a check to be sure that your head is over the top of your spinal core, shift your head rearward (toward your back) 1/8 inch. Maintain a level chin; do not tuck your chin downward or raise it up.

Waiting until later in your form sequence to set your head position is not an option. You'll do it more consistently if you do it now while your muscles are not under tension.

• 25a: Good archery demands erect posture and a level chin. A slight rearward shift of your head will guarantee that your head is directly over the top of your spine.

•25a

The position you have now set puts your head in the best possible position to allow your rhomboids and levator scapulae muscle to work together. If you keep your chin in a protruded or stuck-out position, the levator scapulae muscle will not be electrically stimulated by the brain at the same time as the rhomboids. We need all the help

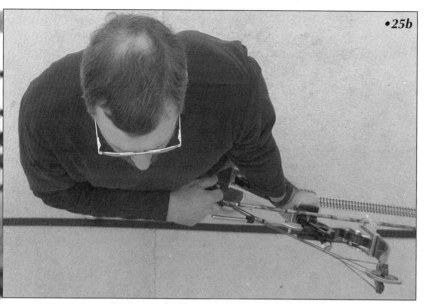

• 25b: Your head must be directly over your spine so the muscle groups of your back will have their maximum leverage.

we can get, so work smarter by keeping your head over your spine so your muscles "fire" at the same time.

I have tested this muscle function with electrodes attached to these muscles groups for a series of shots. Every time I extended my chin, these muscle groups reached peak stimulus at different times. Only when I had my head directly over my spine and my chin level did I get a synchronized firing of all draw-side rhomboid and levator scapulae muscles.

Try your own test by lifting a 20-pound weight in front of you using both hands. Do this with your chin protruded and again with your head directly over your spine. You'll notice how much easier lifting is and how much more stable you are with erect head and shoulder position. Check your golf swing, tennis swing or bowling motion this same way and you'll notice a significant improvement with proper head position. Even Olympic swimmers must use proper head position to get the most from their back muscles.

Once you've set your head over your spine, simply rotate your head **(26)** about 80 degrees toward the target. I'm not sure if you can turn a full 90 degrees. It's not comfortable for me, and I have good range of motion; so let's say 80 degrees. Do not raise or lower your chin during the turn toward the target. Protect this head position for the remainder of the shot to ensure maximum efficiency.

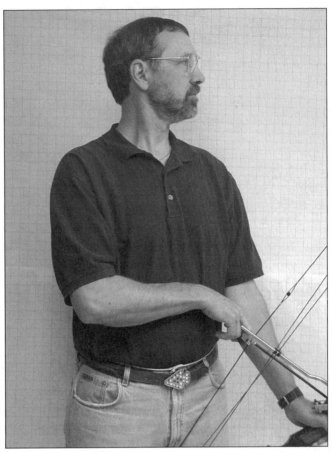

•26: Keep your chin level when you turn to see the target.

RELATION TO SHOOTING OBJECTIVE

This should be obvious. To use back tension means to use rhomboid muscles plus the levator scapulae muscle, and using them together is vital to your consistency. Work on your head position to get the most from these muscle groups. Your archery will improve.

Stand

THE SHOT SEQUENCE IN DIGITAL IMAGES

Seeing is believing. The following digital images will allow you to see the steps of a good archery shot as they are being built. Study the flow from one image to the next to identify how each of the 12 steps leads into the next.

My son, Todd, filmed this 30-second video burst of me shooting a well-executed archery shot. It's not perfect, only the best I could do at the time. To show the shot in this chapter, he chose 44 images (every eighteenth image) from the 800 recorded. These 44 images appear on the bottom right corner of the following odd-numbered pages so you can thumb through them from front to back and see the "video" in action. They worked best by being in the middle of the book.

If you have your own digital camera, you can do the same. Looking at yourself frame by frame is very helpful in finding the good stuff along with the steps that need improving. Save the video on a CD for later reference.

Use video cameras also to film yourself from several angles – front, back, release elbow and top. Watch it over and over to identify the steps that need to be improved. Don't forget to look for the steps you are doing well and reward yourself with a pat on the back for them. Remember, this is supposed to be fun, so always think positive.

CHAPTER THREE
THE DRAW

REVIEW
So far we have:
1) *Set the Stance*
2) *Nocked the Arrow*
3) *Set the Bow Hand*
4) *Set the Release Hand*
5) *Set the Shoulder Posture and Head Position*

The next phase of your shooting form involves getting to full draw position. This must be done in a manner that takes full advantage of what we have already set in place. It also must be done with the final shooting objective in mind.

6. RAISING THE BOW

VISUAL CONTACT
With my head in proper position, I lock onto the target visually. I focus my vision on the target center and never relinquish that focus until the arrow hits the target. This takes practice, but once you master this technique you will stay more in line with the target physical-

30   The Draw

ly. Golfers and baseball players have to keep their eye on the ball (their target), and archers need to keep their eye on the X all the way through the shot and into the follow-through. Look away and you'll shoot away.

How you raise your bow is important because of this act's potential effect on your posture. You must learn to raise your bow by moving only your **(27a, b, c, d)** arm and not your shoulder. Imagine picking up your arm from the wrist without moving your spine or head or changing shoulder position. Ballet dancers do this with a fluid movement; you must do the same to protect your shoulder alignment and head position. Remember that you've set your body position with a specific goal in mind, so don't change it during any part of the shot sequence.

Practice this move without your bow. Learn how it feels before you do it with your bow. Remember that you'll be raising your bow arm and release arm simultaneously without changing your head or shoulder positions. Do it smoothly, without rushing, keeping both arms at the same elevation throughout the raise.

Raising your bow to reach an elevation that places your sight pin three or four inches above the target center is most efficient. If you've been raising it higher to get your bow drawn, you may be drawing too much weight. I recommend lowering draw weight a little until you can draw the bow properly. First, learn to shoot correctly, then increase the draw weight to get more speed; speed can never compensate for poor form.

Both arms should be raised to the same height at the same time. Your draw-side elbow never should be held lower than your bow arm. I see many archers with their drawing elbow held low and close to their body and notice immediately that their drawing shoulder gets out of position. Seldom do they return their draw shoulder to the same level position as their bow-arm shoulder.

To aid the drawing of your bow, rotate your hips several degrees, in the horizontal plane, toward the target as you raise your bow. Don't change your stance, just your body from the hips up **(28 & 29a-d)**. With your upper body more open to the target, you can use your hips and torso to help draw your bow. Just rotate your hips and torso back to their original position as you draw your bow. The best way to do this is to tighten your oblique abdominal muscles during the draw so your entire body works as a unit. Again, decrease the draw weight on your bow so you can learn to do this properly.

RELATION TO THE SHOOTING OBJECTIVE

Shoulder position is the most noticeable connection to executing back tension here. Without both of your shoulders at the same

• *27a, b, c, d: The raising of the bow begins with your bow arm extended and bow hand set and relaxed. Raise your bow arm from below the shoulder ball/socket, not with your shoulder muscles. Continue raising both arms as a unit until your bow is pointed slightly above the target.*

•30a

•30b

•30c

•30d

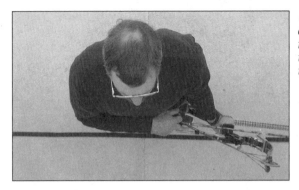

• 28: Your hips are directly over your feet as you prepare to turn your head to the target.

level it is difficult, if not impossible, to get good leverage from your rhomboids. If your rhomboids are only partially effective, then you have to compensate by using the larger back and arm muscles and, as mentioned earlier, that leads to inconsistency and premature fatigue. Maximize your back tension effectiveness by using proper shoulder and head position.

7. THE DRAW

Drawing begins after your bow has reached a level three or four inches above the target center. Your primary vision must be focused on the target center, with the sight pin in your secondary vision. Your draw-side arm and both shoulders are also at this level, and your bowhand is completely relaxed.

With your shoulders, arms and torso working as a connected unit, draw the bow. That means you begin rotating with your hips **(29b)** at the same time as you begin drawing with your arm/shoulder unit. It's easier if you use your body from the hips up to start the draw.

When your hips return to their stance position, continue drawing with your draw-side arm, shoulder and back unit. Your hips should remain in the position you established **(29a & d)** when your stance was set, while you hold both shoulders at the same level.

Many archers I've seen over the years have raised their bow much higher than the target level before they draw. They draw with the bow in this higher position and then lower it to the target. I'm sure many do this so they can draw the higher weight that yields higher speed.

I caution against it because of the potential for shoulder injury. Rotating the shoulder socket under load causes unnecessary wear and tear on the joint and the four rotator-cuff muscles that hold the ball in the socket. These four small muscles provide stability for the ball and socket and when used improperly can be damaged. Without any one of these muscles, stability and function are lost.

• 29a-d: As you begin to draw, you may want to turn your hips a few degrees more toward the target, as shown in (b). Rotate your hips back to their starting position as a way to help you draw your bow. At full draw position (d), your hips should once again be set over your feet.

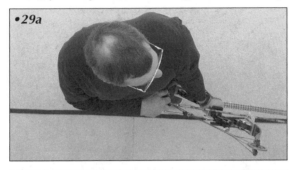

•29a

•29b

•29c

•29d

The Draw

I've had injuries that kept me from shooting for several months. It's no fun wondering if you'll ever shoot again, let alone shoot well. At one point, I could not raise my bow arm enough to put my bow hand in my pants pocket. It took three years of hard work and proper care to regain the form and consistency needed to shoot great scores.

CONNECTION TO THE SHOOTING OBJECTIVE

During the draw stroke, you must also be aware of your line of direction to the target. You've been visually focused on the target center, but have you been drawing your bow close to this line? If you draw your bow in some other line, then you must bring the bow and arrow back to your aiming line to complete the set-up of the shot. Why not avoid the wasted time and energy by drawing close to your line of focus? If you do, you will be better able to maintain upper body position to execute back tension.

8. FULL DRAW POSITION

The draw stroke must be done in a smooth manner with your arms and shoulders held level so you can reach Core Archery full draw position. This is the position where your scapula or shoulder blade is set so you can, at the proper time, increase your back tension to complete the shot release.

Maintaining level shoulders is important for optimum leverage **(30a & b)**. If you raise your drawing shoulder while drawing, then it will be positioned too high to allow the most efficient rhomboid performance. You will also not get the optimum level of assistance from the levator scapula muscle. If these muscles are not giving their optimum level of performance, then other muscles are compensating. That means arm and neck muscles are helping, and fatigue becomes a big enemy again. Can you consistently coordinate all these muscles as well as you can coordinate just a few, and without fatigue? No.

In full draw position, your shoulder blade (scapula) is set near your spine **(30c)** in what you feel is a comfortable position. It should not be as close to your spine as possible but close enough to be secure and stable. You must be able to move your scapula closer to your spine when you make your final contraction of rhomboid and levator scapulae contraction. Full-draw-position is reached when the drawing forearm is in line behind the arrow.

When you reach full draw position, the drawing force is transferred to your shoulder unit and on into your rhomboids. Your forearm muscles, biceps and triceps now can be relaxed so they do not affect the release.

• *30a, b, c: As you draw your bow, your scapula is moved closer to your spine. At full draw, your scapula should be in its optimum position for final back tension execution.*

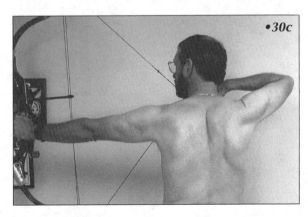

The Draw

Executing back tension demands maintaining rhomboid contraction level when you reach full draw position. When you're drawing a compound bow, you can get trapped into relaxing after you pass peak weight. That's fine for your arm muscles, but you shouldn't relax your rhomboids, levator scapula or trapezius muscles. If you relax your rhomboids, your shoulder blade will not stay in optimum position for final shot execution. If your trapezius relaxes, then your shoulder will not be sufficiently linked to your scapula and back tension fails to produce results.

Maintaining the tension in these muscles is essential for back tension success. In fact, you should continue to increase the contraction level in these muscles. Trying to maintain a steady level is difficult and may lead to a decrease in contraction. **You must, at all cost, avoid any decrease in contraction levels in these back muscles while relaxing your arm muscles.**

When you stop drawing your arrow over the rest, and you reach full draw with your compound bow, you must continue to contract your back muscle groups as noted above.

The recurve archer does not have the luxury of stopping arrow movement across the arrow rest. If he or she is shooting a clicker draw check **(31)** device, that shooter still has several millimeters of arrow to draw after reaching full draw. Stopping is not an option for the good recurve shooter.

The recurve advantage is the fact that you don't pass over peak weight and are never lulled into a relaxed feeling, as you can be with the compound. The smooth increase in draw weight is helpful in completing the aim **(32)** by the time you reach full draw position. The compound archer, on the other hand, must take time to complete the aim after reaching full draw. Both must continue to increase their rhomboid contraction level throughout this time period and up until the arrow is released.

The major difference in the two disciplines is in arrow movement. The recurve archer uses back tension to continue arrow movement across the rest, while the compound archer uses it to change the position of the drawing arm and release hand to activate a mechanical device.

The primary problem with letting back tension decrease is in getting it started again to complete the shot.

To review full draw position, let's look at what you have set in place. Both shoulders and your draw arm are on the same level. Your bowhand is completely relaxed, as are your drawing wrist, forearm and upper arm. After drawing your bow horizontally, you may want to raise your drawing elbow slightly to enhance back muscle leverage while your head remains erect over your spinal column.

The Draw

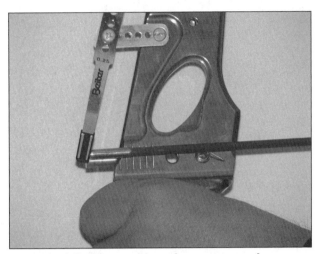

• 31: At full draw position, the recurve archer should have only one millimeter of arrow point under the clicker. Executing the final phase of back tension will draw the point through, and the clicker will signal that it's time to release.

• 32: Many finger and release shooters have a touch point that corresponds to full draw position. This is fine as long as scapula position is the primary focus when setting your full draw position.

The Draw

You visually acquired the target when you first turned your head toward it. Now you must maintain that acquisition until the arrow is released.

Now is the time for you to contact a touch point between your drawing hand and your neck, jaw and/or face. This touch or anchor point is only a secondary reference for full draw position **(32)** and should never be the main focus. To make a point here, when you're asked the location of your anchor point, you should answer "my scapula position", not "my chin" or "my neck".

Your full draw position is complete when you set your scapula and the bow, arrow and sight are brought in line with your view of the target. You are now prepared to complete the next step of your form – aiming.

RELATION TO YOUR SHOOTING OBJECTIVE

By definition, full-draw-position is the prerequisite to back tension. You must set your scapula in the best possible position to complete rhomboid contraction. Consistency at the target peaks when your scapula is set properly, and you use your rhomboids to their best advantage.

CHAPTER FOUR
AIM & RELEASE

REVIEW

So far we have:

1) Set the Stance

2) Nocked the Arrow

3) Set the Bow Hand

4) Set the Release Hand

5) Set the Posture/Head Position

6) Raised the Bow

7) Drawn the Bow

8) Set the Full Draw Position

9. AIM / CONTRACT / AIM

SIGHT LINE-UP

Technically, the aim began when you first visually acquired the target (discussed in more detail in Chapter Seven). Once you have set your full draw position, you must intensify this aiming by involving your sighting devices.

• 33: Raise your bow to a level that places your sight slightly above the intended target.

As you draw the bow, your sight-system reference point (pin or scope) should appear on the upper half of the target **(33)**. Many see it at about 11 o'clock, several inches away from the center. Others prefer it to be at 12 o'clock or 1 o'clock several inches out. You will have to practice this sight presentation position to find what you can do most consistently. At any rate, your sight is in your secondary vision and the target center is occupying your primary visual focus.

By the time you reach full draw position, your sight pin should slide into your primary focus. You've maintained visual contact from the time you visually acquired the target center, and now is not the time to give it away. **Teach yourself to slide the sight into view without changing your point of focus.**

Some archers focus on the target until their sight gets near the target and then switch their vision to the sight. The problem with this maneuver lies in having to reacquire the target center. This takes time and energy at the point in your form sequence when you have little of either to waste.

Consider also that as your vision changes focus, your body will often realign to the new direction. An example of this is the golfer who moves his vision away from the ball just an instant before his clubface hits it. If he looks up, his body follows, the club head is lifted slightly and the ball is hit thin or worse. Understand that we aren't going to dribble an arrow down the floor or into the grass, but our impact point may not be consistent because we haven't paid attention to a fundamental rule of aiming: focusing on the target so our body stays in the best possible line for success. **So, visually lock on to the target center and NEVER let it go.**

Attempting to regain your visual focus must not change your head position. Remember that earlier we set our head in the best possible position for back tension to give the levator scapula muscle it's best chance to synchronize with the rhomboids. If you move your head, you lessen that degree of synchronization.

You can teach yourself to slide the sight pin or scope into view in front of your primary focus. If you're using a peep sight, it, too, must be moved in front of your eye without changing target-center focus.

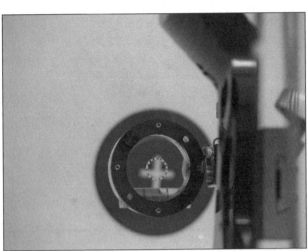

• 34: As you draw, work with gravity to allow your sight to slide down into the middle of the target.

Practice this at close range with a target face, although it's not necessary to shoot. Just practice maintaining focus on the center and bringing the sight pin into your line of sight.

Once the sight lowers into the target center, aiming reaches it's second-highest level. Allowing your pin to settle down into the center **(34)** is crucial to continuing your aiming effectively. If you allow it to fall below the center, then you must expend more energy to get it back up to the center. Train yourself to work efficiently at this point and avoid wasted time and energy.

What you have done so far in establishing the aim is important to the *quality* of aim. Keeping the bow hand, release hand and both arms relaxed is critical to a steady aim. If you tense your bow hand and drawing arm, you will create a nervous and unsteady aim, which leads to uncertainty and more tension in other body parts. In other words, you enter a vicious downward spiral with your aiming, from which you may not recover.

When your pin is seen in the target center with an acceptable degree of steadiness, move to the next step -- signaling the final rhomboid contraction.

RELATION TO YOUR SHOOTING OBJECTIVE

Establishing a relaxed aim increases your chances of a quality aim. When your aim is of good quality on a regular basis, then you can learn to move smoothly to complete back tension. Obviously, smoothness here is of utmost importance to getting your shot completed in a timely manner and achieving the consistency you want at the target.

CONTRACT

The beginning of this final stage of back tension involves the conscious mind. The brain must signal the rhomboids to make the final contraction increase to complete the release, just like a pilot getting clearance for take-off. This conscious signal sets the needed increase into motion and turns the task over to the task-performing (subconscious) mind for completion. Your conscious mind must then focus one hundred percent on aiming.

In full draw position, the scapula is prepared for the final movement toward the spine. This micro-movement is a sliding rotation of the scapula, which pulls the shoulder unit with it. This shoulder movement causes the arm to move in the horizontal plane, which changes the release-hand position. This change in hand position causes the release aid to discharge.

• 35: Further contraction of your rhomboids willcause your draw-side elbow to move perpendicular to the arrow.

Your release-side elbow should move in a horizontal plane. The direction of movement (35) should be perpendicular to the arrow and toward your back. Your elbow cannot move away from the target, since it's attached to your shoulder. Your elbow can't move toward your front side unless your rhomboids get longer. Contracting

rhomboids get shorter, making it physically impossible for elbow movement toward your front side. Therefore, **your elbow must move toward your back a tiny amount. That movement may not be visible.**

The finger shooter uses back tension to continue arrow movement over the arrow rest. This movement is small, maybe 1/16-inch, but it's enough to activate the clicker draw check. Setting full draw position is similar to that of a release shooter, but if you're drawing with your fingers you have to allow a little more room for scapula movement. The movement is the same in either style, but the degree is greater for the finger shooter, due to the need to move the arrow across the rest and through the clicker.

While drawing the bow, you should have been focusing on setting scapula position, then on the sight line-up, and now you must consciously signal the rhomboids to contract further. Again, this is only a signal to begin the final contraction step, and then you must return to focus on the aim and allow your task-performing mind to continue and complete the rhomboid contraction business. Proper training with a tension release aid or clicker is the only way I know to embed this skill in your task-performing mind.

AIM

Moving your conscious thinking back to aiming is important for maintaining a quality aim. Since your conscious mind can focus on only one activity at a time, you had better focus on aiming at the "x" if you hope to hit it. Allowing your mental focus to wander away from aiming will lead to hitting something else, and you don't want that.

To assist my aiming at this final and most intense stage, I use an o-ring sight reticle. Seeing through the o-ring into the target center is consistent with maintaining an unobstructed line-of-sight rather than looking at a dot in front of the center. I find myself moving the dot to the side so I can see the center. You will have to search this out on your own to find which works best for you, but remember that focusing on the target leads to hitting it.

While I'm consciously immersed in this most intense aiming phase, the target center seems to grow. When I'm shooting well, I seem to see the gold or black spot get larger. It's almost as if it's getting closer to me, like a baseball to a batter. It's difficult to explain, but I get the sensation that the world around me is reducing to a small funnel which leads directly to an enlarging x-ring. When I get into this zone, archery is easy because the target is so large. The Zen concept of "becoming one with the goal" comes to mind.

Meanwhile, my task-performing mind is running the rest of my

body. It runs my heart, lungs and back tension. It continues contracting my rhomboids and levator scapula until the release aid activates or the clicker clicks. Training to get this to happen is essentia and happens only as a result of proper practice.

Immersing your conscious mind in aiming and allowing you subconscious to continue back tension leads to the next step - the release.

RELATION TO YOUR SHOOTING OBJECTIVE

This is it! You are now in the midst of reaching your objective You are making the shot happen, and you must complete the aim/contract/aim step without interruption. If you are not deeply consciously focused on aiming, then other events or thoughts may distract you from completing your final objective step. Your mental discipline is being tested to the maximum at this point. Only your determination and practice ethic will carry you through to its completion.

10: RELEASE

When your back tension efforts have caused enough movement your back tension release aid will change angle and activate, releasing the bowstring. This happens as you are immersed in aiming and unaware of when the release will actually occur. That's the rea beauty of shooting with back tension; you have no conscious thought about when the release will occur or about making it go off

If you engage your conscious thinking in setting off the release aid, you have a potential problem. Having to move your conscious mind from aiming to triggering leaves you at a deficit in the aiming department. When that happens, your aim floats or falls off the target center, resulting in missed shots when the release does go off.

Even worse, you may get into a game of anticipation. As you conscious thought moves to triggering, your bow arm anticipate the release of the arrow and moves. This takes only a few hundredths of a second, but that's enough to cause some shots to miss the entire target.

The release aid must be activated through the use of the task-performing mind. If you can do that, your conscious can engage fully in aiming. Results will be maximized.

Aim & Release

11: FOLLOW THROUGH

• 36a & b: A front view before release (36a) and after release (36b) shows a slight backward follow-through movement of the release hand. If your rhomboids are the dominant muscles at work, only a small movement is possible at release.

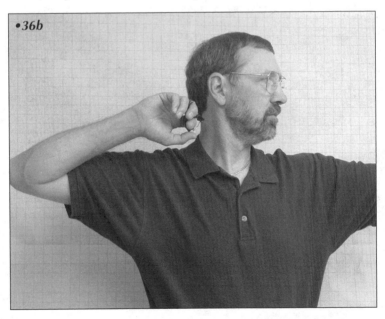

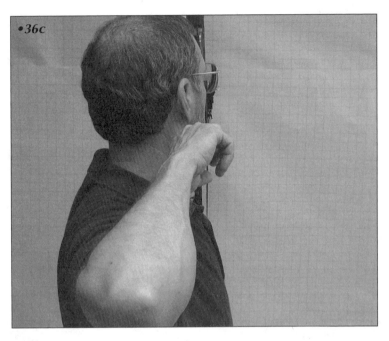

• 36c & d: Rear and top views also show only a small amount of movement at release.

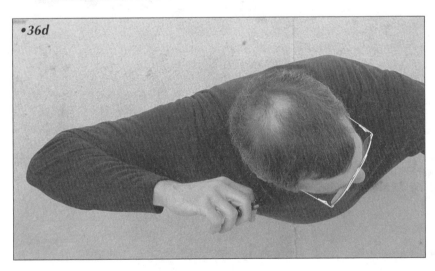

Aim & Release

If you are unaware that the release is going to activate, your relaxed body will act naturally when the release activates. So what is a natural reaction to your release going off or the clicker clicking? Follow-through!

Full-draw position (**36a**), as described earlier, and maintaining a relaxed draw arm dictates that your follow-through movement (**36b, c, d**) will be rather short. You've moved your scapula about as close to your spine as possible during the tightening phase, so your shoulder will not be able to move far when the release lets go. As a result, your release arm cannot fly backward away from the target; a relaxed arm will fall slightly away from the target and slightly downward. A release arm that flies backward (**37**) any great distance is an indication that too much tension is building in biceps and triceps of your drawing arm.

• 37: If you tense some of your arm muscles during shot execution, an unwanted greater movement will occur after release.

Your bow arm, if not tensed, also will fall downward slightly. Sometimes my bow arm stays rather close to target level, but usually it falls six to ten inches downward. A leftward thrust, for right-handers, after the release indicates some unwanted bow-arm tension and, maybe, some upper body and neck tension. Getting relaxed and staying relaxed during shot execution is vital to success and is evidenced by a short, natural follow-through.

XII: SYSTEM RE-SET
The follow-through lasts only a second. When you bring your bow down, you need to review quickly the outcome of your efforts

and evaluate it. Don't get into a beat-yourself-up session; just evaluate your shot and note what you did well or affirm what you need to improve on the next shot. Then, separate yourself from it.

Forget it completely and forever. Learn from it, yes, but don't remember anything else about it, because you have no more control over it. You can control only the shot you are in the process of making, and making a good shot in archery requires your full attention.

Totally separating from a shot is difficult, but you can learn to do it. Carrying the baggage of a previous shot, good or bad, gets heavy after awhile and interferes with making the next shot. Obviously, this is a mental discipline skill that you will need to practice to become good at.

After you've made your evaluation of the shot and separated from it, you need to relax. In fact, this helps you through the separation. Use some sort of relaxation technique, such as a deep breath and long exhale, and then allow your arms to relax. I often close my eyes for this and allow my arms to go limp before touching the next arrow.

When I do touch the next arrow, I must be ready for business. That business is shooting the new arrow using back tension. I must then have all other baggage removed from my mind; reaffirming my shot objective is a good way to do it.

Here's where you must remember that archery is a "now" sport. That means you have control of only one arrow – the one on your string. The others already shot and the ones to come are never affected by how you shoot this one, so don't let them interfere. Think only "this arrow"!

CONCLUSION

This concludes the Core Archery form process. These 12 steps can lead you to higher scores if you practice doing them correctly in the proper order. These steps tell you what to do, how to do it and, most important, when to do it. You must now begin your practice to make it all happen.

Several of the concepts in these 12 steps need more development. They include learning back tension (how the back muscles are working), aiming and sighting. Read the following chapters and learn more on these concepts.

CHAPTER FIVE
LEARNING BACK TENSION

WHY USE A BACK-TENSION RELEASE AID

This chapter will be of great interest to you if you accept my belief that the archery shot must be executed using back tension. It will get you started on your journey toward integrating back tension into your shot sequence.

Because you're reading this chapter, one of two things is probably true – you are not satisfied with the scores you're shooting, or you're not satisfied with the consistency of your form. In either case, you are searching for what it takes to get higher scores or more consistency. The answer, I believe, lies in the concept of back tension and your ability to apply it to archery.

Using back tension is not that difficult to learn, but consistent repetition requires practice. Everybody wants high scores and high consistency, but you must be willing to work to get it. If you apply a solid work ethic to learning and practicing with a back-tension release, it will pay big dividends.

RELEASE DYSFUNCTION (target panic) is another reason for using a tension release. If you have a release dysfunction, you need to invest time and effort into learning how to use a tension release so you can discover how good you can be in archery. You can win with other release aids, but the tension release teaches you to make a

70   Learning Back Tension

"good" archery shot while under full mental and physical control of your body. Then, and only then, will you be equipped to reach your potential.

I remind you here of the Two Steps Of Archery:
Step 1:   Learn to shoot a ten.
Step 2:   Repeat Step One!

This chapter deals with Step Two. You have probably shot many tens by this point in your archery career and are now interested in repeating the shot process at a higher rate. You would like to repeat it more consistently than your competitors and, so, you must acquire the tools to do it.

HOW THE TENSION RELEASE WORKS

The typical tension release has few parts (**38a & b**) and no trigger. The handle can be gripped by two, three or four fingers and holds a "D" shaped metal shear. The shear is used to catch and hold another part – the key or hook – until the release handle rotates several degrees. At a controlled angle of rotation the key slips off the shear, the release rope slips off the hook, and the bowstring is released.

• **38a: The back tension release is simple compared to most. The 'D' shaped ledge is held in place by an axle and set screw. The same axle holds the head so that its key can hook on the 'D'.**

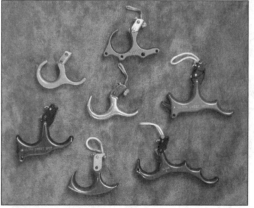

• **38b: Back tension releases come in a variety of shapes and sizes. Some can be drawn with three or four fingers while others are for two fingers only.**

Rotating the handle a few degrees discharges this release and the bowstring. It rotates as the hand holding it changes position and the fingers on that hand maintain tightness. Anyone can make that happen by a simple twist of the wrist, but it can and should happen through the use of back tension, as defined previously.

A top view of an archer at full draw position can quickly demonstrate the movement needed. The elbow of your release arm **(see 35, pg. 56)** must be moved perpendicular to the arrow through the use of rhomboid contraction. Your elbow remains in a horizontal plane during this movement. Because this movement is small, the change in drawing arm and hand position is small, but it does exist and can be harnessed to activate your release aid.

WHY DOES IT SOLVE RELEASE DYSFUNCTION?

Release dysfunction is mental dysfunction. Release dysfunction is the result of unnecessary or inappropriate conscious thoughts occurring at the most inappropriate time – the time just prior to and during release of the arrow. Good archery shots conclude with one picture – aim – being held by the conscious mind. The task-performing mind is operating back tension and all other activities needed to execute the shot. Under these simple conditions your body has the best chance to react properly to shot execution. In other words, **the brain and the body don't know when the shot is going to be released and cannot do anything to adversely affect its execution.**

If some other thought enters this simple little world, then the body can be cued to perform an action that will adversely and uncontrollably affect the shot. Some call this "anticipation". It's only natural that the body reacts to a thought, and so the real problem becomes thought elimination.

Extra thoughts can creep into your archery shot when you use a trigger type release aid **(39a & b)**. At some point in the "aim and tighten" phase of the shot, many think about touching or squeezing the trigger. At that point, your aim and/or your tightening is disturbed. Usually, your bow arm reacts in anticipation, but the tightening of your rhomboids may also be affected. In either case, the shot will be disturbed and the arrow doesn't hit the desired target. Obviously, the "touching/squeezing-the-trigger" thought needs to be eliminated, so the thought process just prior to release is as simple as it can be.

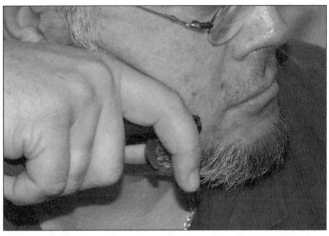

• 39a: Holding your trigger finger near the trigger while aiming will lead to a variety of releasing problems.

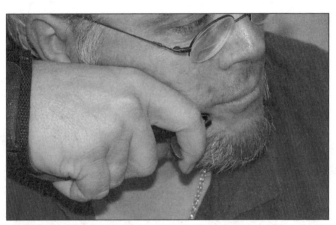

• 39b: Hold your finger around the trigger, making contact with it while aiming. With this method, you have to tighten your finger muscles only while tightening back muscles to get a clean release.

The clicker handles the problem by inserting an audible signal, cueing the archer to activate the trigger quickly to cause shot execution. Finger shooters use the click as a cue to relax their fingers, which allows the string to escape their grasp and launch the arrow.

Some release aids require a relaxation of a finger or fingers to be triggered. This may or may not help the process, as neither of these has to rely on the use of back tension and good body position.

Learning Back Tension

Neither relies on maximizing skeleton and minimizing muscle, which is the secret of consistent archery. The tension release aid relies on both of these principles.

The tension release works mental wonders, because you have the entire handle in your fingers from the beginning of the draw. You don't have to think about touching anything; you're already touching it. You can go about the business of setting proper body position, proper head position, aiming and tightening your rhomboid muscles. Once your body position is established, you can start the aim and tighten process and continue it until, in time, the release parts separate and the string is released. You remain immersed in conscious aiming and subconscious tightening and allow the release aid to determine when the shot will go off. Your conscious-thought process remains efficient and your body is cued to do only those actions that contribute positively to the shot.

STARTING WITH A BACK-TENSION RELEASE AID

Shooting your first arrow with a back-tension release (BTR) aid can be a scary thing; you've probably heard many war stories about archers hitting themselves in the face and mouth while trying to draw a BTR. Not to worry! I have an easy, pain-free method for starting people on a BTR, so just read on.

Using a six-foot piece of 1/8th-inch nylon rope (**40**), tie the two ends together to form a loop equal in length to your bow's draw length. Place one end of the loop around your bow hand as shown while hooking your BTR to the other end (**41**) as you would hook it to your bowstring. Now the loop acts as your bow, and you can reproduce your full-draw body position without drawing the bow and without any threat of bodily harm.

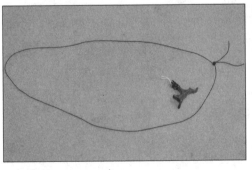

• **40: Use a rope loop in place of your bow when you need frequent practice with your back-tension release aid. Be sure to adjust the loop to your draw length.**

Learning Back Tension

• 41: Practice proper body position for every 'practice shot' you take with your loop/release system.

Adjust the length of the rope to match your bow's draw length so you feel comfortable. In other words, adjust it to match your full-draw body position. That means your shoulders must be level, your dominant-side scapula in position to begin back tension, drawing elbow slightly raised above level, and your bow arm extended to allow the force of your tension to be carried by bone structure. Body position is all-important to form, so, even with this rope, practice it right.

Once you're in proper position, relax your drawing-side arm muscles. Remember that this is easiest when your draw-wrist is kept straight and forearm muscles are relaxed. Also, consistent archery form minimizes muscle and maximizes skeleton.

Now is the time to start tightening your draw-side rhomboids. As they tighten, you will feel your arm, elbow, release hand and BTR move, too. Eventually, the BTR will release the rope loop and the bowstring.

BE PATIENT! DO NOT RUSH THIS PROCESS!
If your BTR goes off too quickly, set it heavier. Learn to use it set heavy so you have to expend much energy and time to get it to go off. Working hard at this stage will get you accustomed to waiting for the release to do its magic. Even if your personality is such that you can't stand waiting, train yourself to wait. Waiting is a habit you can learn.

When you are executing with back tension properly, the rope loop will launch four or five feet outward. If, when released, it just hangs around your bow hand (42) you're not using any tension and simply turning the release handle with your wrist or fingers. Learn how it's done and how it feels in your back; keep doing it until it is transferred to your task-performing mind.

Learning Back Tension

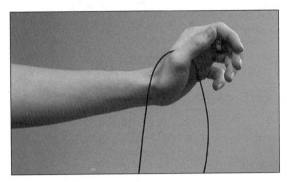

● 42: If you don't generate any back tension with your release, the rope will not launch forward out of your hand. Instead, it will just fall limply around your thumb as shown.

This rope and the BTR can be used anywhere, anytime. Practice with it in your office, living room, basement, on business trips or anywhere you are. Use it for, maybe, 20 shots at a time. More shots per practice session are not necessary, but more practice sessions are. Practice four or five times a day, because frequent review promotes long-term retention of the skill being practiced. These frequent sessions will also help with muscle conditioning and mental control. Be sure to review body position with each practice session.

SELECTING A BACK-TENSION RELEASE AID

The back-tension release has been around since the early 1970s when Mel Stanislawski invented it. I started using one in 1977 and haven't been able to put it down since. On the urging of a friend, I borrowed his "Stan" for a test run. He never got it back.

From the first shot, I knew I was a better archer. With my Stanislawski, the arrow groups were good and got better and better, until I was shooting well from all distances. My first indoor scores that winter were over 590 on the 40cm FITA target, and I was impressed with how this release aid **(43)** had changed me.

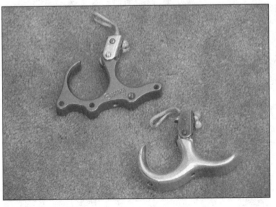

● 43: The silver release is my old favorite. It probably has a million shots on it. The inventor, Mel Stanislawski, gave the other one to me.

I've used other releases, but I keep going back to the BTR. With it, I can maintain my form. Without it, I quickly fall into a lazy mode with my back tension, and the groups in the target get bigger.

Back-tension releases are available from several manufacturers. Models for two, three and four fingers are shown. I know all the manufacturers personally and have tried all of these products. I urge you to try them in an effort to find the one that best fits your hand and improves your consistency. Over the years, I've had the most success with a two-finger Stanislawski but a three- or four-finger model may better serve you.

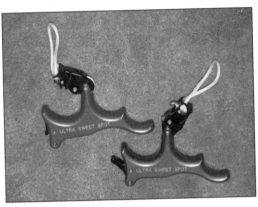

• **44: On the left, the TRU Ball Sweet Spot release-head is free-floating, while on the right the thumb button has been engaged to lock the head to the handle. This safety mechanism opens the way for many new archers to try back tension without fear of premature discharge.**

• **45: Carter Releases produces a full line of back-tension release aids. From the lower-left and clockwise are the Atension 4, Colby Hinge, at the top is the Solution 2.5 2-finger, Solution 2.5 4-finger and the Atension 2.**

SAFE DRAW

If you're concerned about your release going off on the draw stroke, try the TRU BALL Sweet Spot release **(44)**. The head of this model is hinged and rotates freely during the draw stroke; no matter what angle you turn the handle, the release won't go off. At full draw, you can press a thumb button to link the handle and head

Learning Back Tension

together, and from that point on you can use your back tension to activate the release. This release really takes the worry out of drawing a BTR. Carter also makes releases with a safety feature.

No matter which model you choose, keep hand position in mind. You must be able to hold the release while keeping your large knuckles and wrist straight. This is the best way to ensure that your forearm muscles are relaxed during the shot.

USING THE BACK-TENSION RELEASE WITH A BOW

When you're ready to use your BTR with your bow, begin at close range, say five yards, with no target and no sight. Your goal is to get the bow to full draw position, aim and reproduce the shot form that you've been practicing with the rope loop. Don't set the release light; heavy is better for training. You know when you're cheating, so don't cheat! Only perfect practice makes perfect.

Frequent short practice sessions each day is, again, the best way to train. Do this for 20 days, because it takes 20 days to build a habit. The goal of each session is to shoot 10 to 15 shots with perfect form and execution.

In time, you'll be ready for a sight and a target. Don't rush to get to them; remain patient and focus on the feel of your body as it sets off the release. Add the sight and a target and shoot at close range. Practice often during the day and only for 10 to 15 shots at a time.

Once again, your goal with this practice is to get to full draw position in order to begin aiming and tightening your rhomboid muscles. Following that, you must remain consciously immersed in aiming while your task-performing mind controls the rhomboid tightening. No other thought is necessary, since the release will eventually go off. Your task, and it's a big one, is just to let it happen.

FURTHER PRACTICE

Once you've begun shooting at targets, you must continue practice with the rope loop and with your sightless bow and no target. Use the loop anytime you can for a few shots. Warm up with it before shooting. Use blank-bale practice before and after each target practice session. Eight or ten shots at the start and eight or ten at the end of every practice session reinforce body position, body feel and, most of all, the mental focus and control that you need to shoot properly.

CHAPTER SIX
MUSCLE ACTIVITY DURING BACK TENSION

For years, I wondered how back tension worked. I didn't know what muscles were contracting or which ones were relaxing. To get answers to these questions, I worked with Guy R. Schenker, D.C. Dr. Schenker is a chiropractor and extremely knowledgeable about the skeletal and muscular function of the body, having worked with athletes from many sports through the past 20 years.

By watching me shoot arrows, Dr. Schenker was able to analyze the movement I was using to activate my release aid. He identified the rhomboids and levator scapulae muscle groups as the primary muscles creating movement in my scapula. My education on back tension had its beginning.

I then taught Dr. Schenker how to use the release aid with a 30-inch loop of rope instead of a bow. He was able to take this with him for a week and study further what he felt in his own body. His conclusions were unchanged, with the added fact that the trapezius was also contracting, connecting the shoulder to the scapula. This connection caused the release arm and hand to change position and activate the release aid.

This insight to back tension has been invaluable to me in further studying how best to implement and teach archers to use it. I

thank Dr. Schenker for his valuable information and am glad to pass it along to you.

In February of 2000, my daughter Jennifer (two-time National Field Archery Champion) graduated from Palmer College of Chiropractic and began her own practice in Naperville, Illinois. In our discussions of shooting form, she has confirmed what Dr. Schenker and I have concluded about back tension and agrees that the rhomboids and levator scapulae muscle are the major contributors to good archery form. I'm sure there is more to learn on this vital subject, and with her help and the help of good friend and bowhunter Dr. Tony Marrara, I'll have more information for you in the coming years.

One big question remained: Could I somehow measure this muscle activity using today's technology? If I could, then no one could doubt the opinions and insights given above. To make a long story short, I had the opportunity to do just that while coaching in Israel. The results are presented in the following pages.

BACK TENSION REVIEW

In Chapter 1, I defined back tension as "the appropriately timed contraction of the rhomboid muscles, aided by the levator scapulae muscle, which results in the micro-sliding rotation of the scapula and shoulder unit **(46)**. The outcome of this motion is the release of the bowstring".

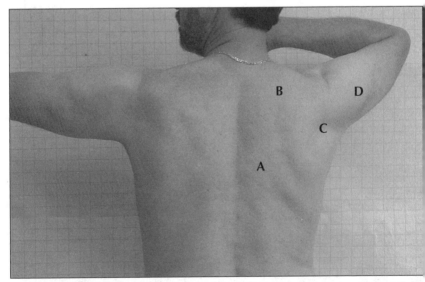

• **46: Four sensors were placed on important muscle groups. Group A is the rhomboids; Group B is the levator scapulae/trapezius; Group C is the infraspinatus, and Group D is the triceps.**

Muscle Activity During Back Tension

Muscle activity can be measured electronically with EMG equipment. **Figure 47** shows the results I obtained while shooting the compound bow with a back-tension release aid.

I was assisted in this effort by physical therapist Yitzak Friedman, Tel-Aviv, Israel. We were both working at the Keshet Eilon Violin Master Course held each summer in northern Israel. I coach archery for the violinists every afternoon to augment their playing form. Yitzak gives them therapy for their physical stress.

Since he was concerned about which muscles the violinists were using to play violin and to shoot archery, we got our heads together for a little experiment. He had the EMG equipment and the knowledge to interpret the results, and I had the archery know-how and shooting ability. He deserves the credit for helping me attach numerical values and times to the muscle contraction levels shown below. I thank him for his valuable assistance.

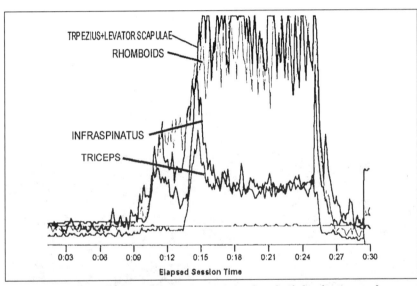

• 47: *The EMG printout shows the activity level of the four muscle groups during a typical shot. Note that the triceps relaxed while the rhomboids continued to elevate in activity until the release occurred.*

WHAT WAS MEASURED

As I understood it, when the compound bow is drawn, the rhomboids, levator scapulae, trapezius and deltoid muscles should be employed, along with arm muscles. When the draw stroke passes peak weight, the force load on the bowstring reduces and the drawing force should be transferred, to the greatest extent possible, to rhomboids and levator scapulae. Following the draw stroke and

set-up in full-draw position, you begin an aiming period during which both the rhomboids and levator scapulae must be contracted to a higher degree in order to complete the release.

To know for sure if this was happening, I needed to measure the level of electric activity in four muscle groups **(47)**. Compared to other levels of electricity, these are quite low but can be sensed by EMG equipment. The EMG measures electrical impulses.

We used four electrodes attached to the following muscle groups on my right, or drawing, side:

A) rhomboids,

B) upper trapezius and levator scapulae,

C) trapezius and infraspinatus, and

D) mid deltoid and triceps.

These four groups give enough information to demonstrate what should happen during shot execution.

We tested several bow raisings and draw strokes to verify and set the EMG parameters. I then drew my bow, aimed and released using a back-tension release aid. The EMG simultaneously measured the electrical activity of the four muscle groups.

I then executed seven good shots, taking my time so the print-out would be spread over 20 seconds and easy to read. The print-outs for all seven were identical to the one shown. Following is an explanation of the results.

HERE'S WHAT HAPPENED

3 seconds: I begin to draw the bow, and all muscles increase in activity level except group D, the mid-deltoid/triceps group.

4 seconds: Group D begins to increase in activity as peak weight is reached.

6 seconds: Peak weight is passed, and a small reduction in activity can be noted in groups C and D, while groups A and B continue to increase.

9 seconds: I've reached full draw position, and all muscle groups are highly active, although groups C and D begin to reduce.

12 seconds: Groups C and D are only half as active as groups A and B. Groups A and B continue to be highly active throughout the aim period.

19 seconds: The release activates, and groups A and B relax instantly.

20 seconds: All groups show relatively low levels of activity.

INTERPRETING THE RESULTS

While many muscles were used to draw the bow and set full-draw position, only the rhomboids and levator scapulae muscles

were used to cause the release. They worked together to move my scapula, shoulder and arm to cause the tension-release aid to activate. The triceps muscle and infraspinatus relaxed after the draw, reducing the level of arm muscle tightness that, in turn, promotes consistency.

CONCLUSIONS

The most important thing you can gain from this information is the level of rhomboid activity you need to attain, and when to attain it. It must rise as the bow is drawn, since this is where the transfer of power to the rhomboids begins.

After passing peak weight, rhomboid activity level must continue to elevate, even as you reach full draw position. At this point, the entire holding force is transferred from your arm muscles to your rhomboids and levator scapulae. Don't fall into the trap of the compound bow and relax this activity level; instead continue to increase it throughout the aiming process until the release aid activates and the string is released.

Many archers relax their back tension after passing peak weight, then activate the release by some means other than back tension. That usually means they use their arm muscles, biceps and triceps, which are not as consistent. Consistency in archery requires minimum use of muscle, and the muscles you do use should be the short rhomboids in your back.

CHAPTER SEVEN
AIMING and SIGHTING

Target archery, 3-D archery and bowhunting all require the skills of aiming and sighting. This begins in Step 5 of your shooting form, as you've already read, but let me explain the difference between aiming and sighting.

Aiming, as I see it (no pun intended), is the act of visually acquiring the intended target spot. Sighting occurs when you involve a reference device(s) such as a sight pin, scope and/or peep sight in your aiming.

To do it right, you always should begin aiming before sighting, continuing it into your follow-through and after the sight pin has left your view. I train myself, and teach my students, to visually acquire the center of the target in Step 5 of their form sequence. By the end of Step 8, the sight has joined the aiming process by sliding in line with your eye's view of the target.

BETTER AIMING YIELDS ALL-AROUND SUCCESS

Learning good aiming and sighting habits will make all your archery better. You can increase scores in your target shooting with better discipline in aiming, and improve your success in hunting, if you use your improved aiming skills.

Many times, while shooting, we get too wrapped up in scoring

and forget the basics of aiming. Knowing what these basics are, and then training yourself to use them, are keys to greater success.

AIMING AND SIGHTING

As I already have mentioned, aiming begins when you visually connect with the target center. Step 5 in your form sequence sets your body and vision in line with the target. Once oriented to that center point, you should never give up visual contact with it. If you do, you risk losing your body alignment with the target, which compromises overall form.

Make yourself a note here that you're not just looking at the target in general, you're looking at the small spot you intend to hit. You lock onto it and see nothing else in your primary vision.

Next, you must raise the bow into the sighting position **(48)**. Here you will, in your secondary vision, see your sighting device just above the target center. Your primary focus remains on the center of the spot.

• 48: Raise your bow so the sight is positioned just above the target center.

While maintaining visual focus on the target spot, draw your bow. You should be able to draw and settle into full draw position without losing visual contact with the spot. If your bow's draw

weight is too heavy, you may not be able to do this. If drawing causes you to lose visual contact with the center for any reason, you'll need to make some changes, such as lowering the draw weight.

Once you reach your full draw position, slide your sight device into your primary view of the target spot **(49)**. Don't look to the sight and then try to reacquire the spot, as this tends to realign your body away from your aiming line. Just slide the sight into your established aiming line.

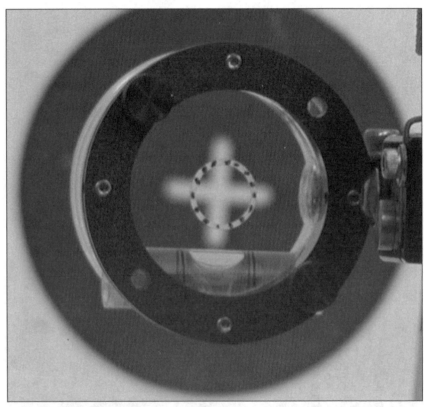

• **49: Sighting begins when the sight pin or scope slides into your primary view in the center of the target.**

Now you're aiming and sighting. You have both your body and your bow lined up as a unit and are totally – visually and physically – focused on the small spot you want to hit.

Finish the shot by doing what you do to execute the release of the bowstring. It is hoped you use back tension, and during this execution you never lose visual focus on your target. Aiming focus con-

tinues throughout the release and into your follow through; it ends when the arrow falls into your view of the target center.

AIMING BETTER

Several physical conditions affect your ability to relax, which, in turn, affects aiming:

A) bow fit,
B) sight picture,
C) body position,
D) physical conditioning, and
E) the state of your conscious mind.

Optimizing these conditions will enable you to aim better and thereby improve your scores.

A) BOW FIT

Draw length, draw weight and grip compatibility affect how well or poorly the bow fits you. You must be sure to make the proper adjustments to all three to optimize your aiming.

I usually start by adjusting draw length of my own new bows or when working with a new student. Getting the draw length right allows me to set full draw position correctly and comfortably. If it's too short, I won't get my draw-shoulder properly positioned for my arm to relax. A long draw length will put me in an overextended position with my scapula already as close to my spine as it can get. Getting it right is vital to establishing proper form.

To search out your optimum draw length, try shooting your bow over a wide range of adjustments. Start with the draw length too short. Adjust it by 1/8- or 1/4-inch increments across a one-inch span until you find your optimum length – the length that allows you to use your scapula properly and consistently.

A strong visual indicator of proper full draw position is the position of your draw-side forearm. It should, at full draw, appear to be an extension of the arrow. **(35)**

Draw length can be adjusted by using string anchor pins or cable anchor pins, or by adding or deleting twists in your bowstring or cables. You also may have a rotating wheel module that allows for small adjustments. Switching one-inch modules is not a bad idea either, as this will tell you rather quickly if you're on the correct module before you make fine adjustments.

If you have to make a shorter or longer string to change draw length, do it. Get the draw length right so you can take full advantage of your Core Archery shooting form.

Do the same with draw weight. Start high or low and make small adjustments until you find your upper and lower limits. Don't let the

bow dictate what you should do with your form. If you can't shoot 70 pounds (and I can't), don't force it on yourself. Instead, change arrow sizes and get comfortable with a lower weight.

When you get draw length set to within 1/8-inch and draw-weight set to the pound, you'll find your aiming ability is improved because you're now more comfortable. More comfort means better relaxation, and that translates to better aiming.

B) SIGHT PICTURE

When you aim, eye performance reaches its maximum level. This performance level involves placing one object – the target – in line with a front sight and a peep sight. With these three at different distances, only one can be in focus. Which one? That's the question you have to deal with, and how you answer it can make aiming more or less difficult.

My solution has almost always been to use a circular aiming reticle **(50)**. My eye tends to center the ring in my scope, with the rings or spot on the target. Of course, if you're shooting 3-D animals, you may not be able to see the circular scoring rings. Even so, I still like seeing the circular reticle on the animal, because it gives me a top-bottom reference on the animal's body.

• 50: My eye tends naturally to center an aiming "ring". The lighting at the Atlantic City Classic was such that I had to add a few black dots to the aiming ring to give it more contrast on the target gold.

Aiming and Sighting

At any rate, you need to find the reticle that puts your eye at ease while you're aiming. The less tension your eye has to endure, the less tense you become. Eye tension can lead to squinting, contorting your facial muscles, and eventually to tightening neck and shoulder muscles.

Some factors to consider are: size and color of your aiming reticle, whether it's a circle or a dot, the magnification power of your scope, the diameter of your scope or pin sight, the distance between the sight and your eye, size of the hole in your peep sight, and the hat you wear to shade your eyes. You must experiment with all these to find what works best for you in all light conditions.

One note about color and vision. I'm far sighted. I can't focus well on close objects, which means I can't see some colors clearly. Orange and red are not what I want to use in my scope or on my pin sights. Colors such as blue and green and yellow work better for me. After learning this, I switched my scope-aiming ring to yellow with good success.

You can test for your best color by using your hunting sight. Most fiber optic sights come with three colored pins – green, yellow and red. Test your vision with these after sunset as the sky darkens. The pin you see the best in twilight is the one you should use all the time. Check with your optometrist to learn which color might be best for you.

C) BODY POSITION

Establishing proper body position can improve your ability to relax. The focus of Core Archery on using the spine to its best advantage conversely is geared to using as little muscle as possible. When you use very little muscle to shoot archery, you can be more relaxed, which in turn improves your aiming.

If you agree that unused muscle can be relaxed, then you have only to relax it, right? Unfortunately, it's not as easy as it sounds. Spending some time learning to relax is a must if you want to improve your relaxation level and then your accuracy.

D) PHYSICAL CONDITIONING

If your heart is pounding, it's more than a little difficult to calm the whitecap waves in your scope bubble. If you're breathing so hard you can barely draw your bow back, it's also difficult to aim. What do you do? My answer is to get in shape for archery by doing a few simple but effective exercises.

1) Walking: Walking is one of the best activities. Making the time – 30 minutes – to walk two miles on alternate days is the difficult part. In fact, if you could walk every day, or five days a week,

• 51: Walking, biking or running on the road or treadmill are great for improving cardiovascular performance.

you'd be better fit for life in general. Your archery would improve, too, because you could better handle the pressure moments of shooting. Getting your pulse and respiration under control will give you great confidence at the beginning and end of any competitive round.

If you want, elevate your walking to some mixed treadmill walking/running **(51)**, or work out on a stationary bike. This training, 30 minutes three or four times a week, will improve your heart and respiration rates while not pounding your legs and back like running on a road surface does. Obviously, you can do the bike and treadmill regardless of the weather.

2) Pulling Arrows: Your upper body needs a workout on right and left sides. We often forget our non-dominant or bow-arm side,

• 52: Pulling arrows with your non-dominant side is a simple way to condition muscles you don't use much and rest those you do.

Aiming and Sighting

and it remains underdeveloped. Some simple exercises can help develop your non-dominant side and prevent injuries.

You can make simple changes to your shooting routine to improve your non-dominant side strength. Pulling arrows with your bow arm **(52)** is the first exercise that comes to mind. In two or three weeks you significantly can increase the strength in your bow arm, bow shoulder and oblique abs by pulling arrows with that side of your body. Just remember to contract all those muscles, not just your arm muscles, when pulling; using more of your body makes it easier and conditions more muscles.

3) Drawing Your Bow: Drawing with your bow arm is another simple exercise that yields great results. Start with a lightweight bow and a few draws before and after each practice session. Gradually, you'll be able to increase that to 20 draws before and after practice.

Another advantage of this exercise is the rehearsal you get with your shooting form. Paying attention to your body position while drawing with your non-dominant side can help you focus and better feel what you do with your dominant side. Build correct form on both sides; don't take shortcuts anywhere.

4) Walking Stick Exercises: While you're walking, you can be doing upper body exercises with your walking stick. Cut a stick about 80 percent of your body length and one-and-a-half to two inches in diameter. It can be thicker at one end, if you like, or you can use a long shovel handle or broomstick.

While walking, I focus on strengthening my bow arm side while stretching and extending my drawing side. The following exercises will do the same for you.

Some points to remember: Holding the thin end is more difficult; hold the stick so the stick weight is manageable; hold it closer to the end as you get stronger; maintain complete control while moving the stick slowly through exercises **a-g**.

a) Side Swing (53): Hold one end of stick, extend arm forward with stick pointed away like a golf club, swing arm/stick horizontally through 150 degrees and back to starting point. Repeat 20 times, then switch arms. Repeat both arms for 20 more reps or do bow arm 20 + draw arm 20 + bow arm 20.

b) Front Vertical Swing (54a & b): Hold one end of stick, extend arm forward below horizontal with stick pointed away, raise arm/stick vertically through 90 degrees and back to start. Repeat as in **a**.

c) Side Vertical Raise (55): Hold one end of stick, extend arm to your side below horizontal, raise to 30 degrees from vertical and lower back to start. Repeat as in **a**.

d) 45-Degree Front Raise A (56): Hold one end of stick, palm down and off center. With the stick horizontal and perpendicular to

• 53: Hold the walking stick near one end. Extend it in front of you and sweep it horizontally. Do it slowly, with maximum control.

• 55: Raise and lower the stick to your side, but don't force it to a high angle.

• 54a & b: With the stick extended in front of you, slowly raise and lower it 20 times.

• 56: With your palm down, hold the stick about one foot from the small end and raise and lower it slowly. Resisting the torque force will help strengthen the rotator cuff muscle group.

• 57: Repeat the palm-down exercise with the large end of the stick to the rear. Now you can resist the torque in the opposite direction.

Aiming and Sighting

•58a

•58b

• *59: You also can practice your golf swing a little to loosen your back muscles. Swing easily at first, then gradually increase the range and velocity.*

•58c

• *58a, b, c: Finish your exercises with single-arm free swings to the side. Do both right and left.*

arm, extend arm at 45 degrees from front, raise to near 10 degrees from vertical and back down. Repeat as in **a**. Resist the clockwise gravitational pull of the heavy end.

e) 45-Degree Front Raise B (57): Do as in **d**, with the stick flipped 180 degrees in your palm-down hand. Resist the counter-clockwise gravitational pull of the heavy end.

f) Free Swing (58a, b, c): Hold one end of stick, swing the stick freely, easily and horizontally or as a golf club. Gradually extend range with each swing. Do 20-30 reps, twice for each arm or more for draw arm.

g) Golf Swing (59): Hold one end of stick with both hands, as you hold a golf club. Swing slowly, freely, as though hitting a golf ball. Swing both directions with increased force during each of 20-30 swings with the last 10 at 80 percent of maximum. Maintain grip control.

E) YOUR CONSCIOUS MIND

Better aiming requires better focus of your conscious mind on the act of aiming. In fact, it should be totally focused on aiming if you want the best results.

If you want the total focus of your conscious mind to be on aiming, then you understand that your task-performing mind must run all the activities needed to cause the release of the arrow. Practicing at a blank bale does this. Working on each part of your form while not aiming will commit the form element to your task-performing mind.

As I mentioned in Chapter 4, using back tension to cause the release of the arrow is important because of the thoughts you **don't** have while aiming. Many archers are caught in the circumstance of having consciously to think about touching the trigger at the time of release and, therefore, lose conscious contact with aiming. Proficiency with back tension allows your conscious mind to signal a further contraction of your rhomboids and then turn that contraction over to the task-performing mind for completion. This done, the conscious mind can focus totally on aiming until the arrow is released.

This all works because back tension is not completed instantaneously. It requires some time, several seconds in fact, to complete. This is plenty of time for the conscious mind to get deeply involved in aiming.

Do you remember the old Chinese proverb "Man who chases two rabbits catches neither"? If you maintain the single goal of aiming for your conscious mind, then you are more likely to attain that goal. Focus consciously on aiming; your aiming will get steadier and more consistent.

Of course, you must have all form elements in place for this to happen. Get busy in front of the blank bale and start working through the steps of Core Archery.

CONCLUSION

Successful archery demands a complete package of skills. The 12 steps of Core Archery make that complete package. You must learn these physical steps first and then work on your mental steps. With Core Archery, you know what to do, how to do it and, most important, when to do it.

CHAPTER EIGHT

THE MENTAL GAME
of CORE ARCHERY

Having the best form is not enough. You must have the mental skills necessary to apply that form at crunch time. To reach your full archery potential, you must learn all that is required of your mind.

As I have experienced it, the mental game means the "conscious mind" applied to the making of a shot. I have been able to compete at the highest level in archery by using my entire natural, given physical and mental abilities to master my own shooting action. Logic has dictated to me that if I take care of "my archery shot" then my score will take care of itself and, win or lose, I can accept my result.

So, continue on and read my thoughts on thinking in the game of archery. It should help your shooting.

THREE MIND FUNCTIONS

There are at least three mind-use functions in archery:

1) One of those mental functions gets used in **recreational archery**;

2) another mind function is involved when we want to **learn to shoot** archery with a specific set of skills in a prescribed order,

3) the third function is needed when we want to **maximize our performance** in a competitive round or hunting shot.

The recreational function involves entertaining yourself, passing the time or just plain playing. It takes no great amount of thought or focus just to shoot some arrows and enjoy it. You aren't following a tightly controlled set of steps, and the result is of no consequence.

Boy, do I like this part of archery. Some of my favorite memories come from those times as a young boy growing up in rural Pennsylvania when I would take my fiberglass bow and just shoot arrows. I liked to watch them fly. I didn't consider how I was holding the bow, releasing the string or any of that stuff. I really didn't think much at all. I just shot arrows, and it was pure fun. In fact, the purest, so every now and then I do just that with my recurve bow.

Somewhere along the way, though, I began to expect more than just flight. I expected to hit something ... something like that old Tide box stuffed with cardboard. At that point, I entered a second function of mind-use. That's when I began consciously or cognitively to think about my form, how to make it better and more consistent. I began actively to impose my conscious thoughts on my body with the intent of gaining more form consistency.

By this time, my dad had gotten involved in archery, and, together, we shot at local clubs. We made archery friends and, of course, being archers, we "helped" each other with our shooting. It was like the proverbial blind leading the blind as we struggled with what was good and what was bad. By trial and error, we improved.

I became good enough to set some scoring records at summer scout camp and win some trophies at local tournaments. We even went to the Pennsylvania Target Championships. I remember finishing poorly, having recently put a sight on my bow for the first time (there was no division for barebow in the youth group). I remember, also, having a fire inside me because I knew I could do better. Deep inside, I knew I could win at archery.

Dad and I continued to shoot tournaments, indoors and out, for years. We read a small booklet called "Power Archery" by Dave Keaggy. Again, spurred on by good information, we imposed our conscious mind on our shooting form, made changes, practiced and became a little better.

I wasn't, however, good enough to take a deer. I remember one October morning in 1960 when I shot all five of my arrows at deer, found and retrieved three of them and shot two of those at more deer, only to be empty handed at the end of the day. Again, the fire burned inside. I knew I could do better. The empty tag made that obvious.

Now, many years later, I know what I needed to do then. Hindsight is, indeed, 20/20. I needed to impose my conscious thinking on my shooting form, but I didn't have a clue about how to do it in a manner that would get results. Beyond that, I also didn't have a clue about what to do with my conscious thinking during a competitive round or that all-important hunting shot. I didn't know how to use that third mind function, the function that lets your body perform a learned activity with near mechanical consistency.

Now I know how to use my mind, at least the part I haven't yet lost.

YOU CAN DO IT, TOO!

THE PREMISE

To move your archery beyond the recreational level, you must know and do the following: **To reach your full archery potential, you must bring your conscious mind fully to bear <u>ON</u> and then <u>WITHIN</u> the act of shooting.**

Yes, there are two mental functions that you must employ to become a better archer.

The remainder of this chapter is presented in two sections:
• **Mental Function 2 – "How to Practice",**
• **Mental Function 3 – "The Competition Mind".**
(Remember, Mental Function 1 is simply recreation.)

Reading these two sections will give you a plan – the Core Archery Mental Plan – for higher performance archery.

THREE MENTAL FUNCTIONS

FUNCTION	CONSCIOUS (THINKING) MIND	TASK PERFORMING MIND	OUTCOME
RECREATIONAL 1	LOW-ACTIVE CONTROL	LOW-ACTIVE PERFORMING	LOW, ERRATIC RETENTION
LEARNING 2	**HIGH-ACTIVE CONTROL**	**ACTIVE LEARNING**	NEURAL LINKS FORMED, MOTOR ACTIONS CONDITIONED AND RETAINED
HIGH PERFORMANCE 3	**COOPERATIVE MONITOR**	**HIGH-ACTIVE PERFORMING**	LEARNED MOTOR ACTIONS REPEATED CONSISTENTLY

The preceding diagram helps illuminate the three mind functions I have thus far described. It shows how two different brain facets – the conscious mind and the task-performing mind – relate during these three different mental functions. Knowing these relationships can help you understand how to shoot and score better.

The interactions are explained in detail in the following two sections of this chapter.

DEVELOP A MENTAL PLAN

Many years ago, I developed a tournament mental plan that worked for me – "Shoot Your Form". I trained myself to think about my form when I got into those especially meaningful situations called tournaments.

The plan wasn't sophisticated or the best plan, but it worked, because my form is what got me tens in practice, which gave me confidence that it also should get tens in tournaments.

Thus, twenty-some years ago, as I focused on my form, I didn't realize how important the thinking part of my game really was to my success. I felt lucky that I had a working plan and thought that was all I needed to know. I couldn't explain all that I was doing, but I knew it was working in most tournament situations.

You need a plan, too. You need and can build a much better plan than I used back then, so keep these words in mind:

"If you fail to plan, then you plan to fail!"

Read on and begin to make your own plan for mental shooting success.

Mental Function 2
LEARNING
Imposing your conscious thinking "<u>ON</u>" the shooting act

With the right purpose and the right application of your mental functions, you can become a significantly better archer. Mental Function 2 utilizes your conscious or thinking mind to focus on individual form steps so your task-performing mind can learn each step in its proper place in your 12 form-steps.

Not only must you learn those steps, you must retain that learning in your brain's neural links. That takes time.

It takes each of us different amounts of time to learn a given task, but as a rule of thumb I use 20 days in this chapter. You may need more than that or less than that. Just be aware that there is no magic in the number 20. You will have to find your own learning time and stick to it.

Obviously, we all learn through practice. Practice, however, is not just shooting arrows. Practice has to be organized and purposeful. To get anywhere, you <u>MUST</u> practice with a purpose.

SOME QUESTIONS TO ANSWER
Can you answer these questions about yourself?
1) Did I practice last Wednesday?
2) What did I accomplish?
3) What score did I have?
4) What part of my form did I work on?
5) What bow tuning did I do?
6) Am I better now than I was a month ago?

If you are serious about elevating your shooting ability, then, of course, you know the answers to all these questions. You know them because you know how to build a practice session properly and make notes to track your progress ... and then you do them!

If you can't answer these questions, as I couldn't at one time, then you need to get busy planning your next practice session.

Many years ago I started a notebook because I was tired of spinning my wheels, relearning the same lessons every week. I became tired of not remembering what bow tuning I did last week or last month, and I became tired of redoing combinations that I had already tried and rejected.

At first it was just notes about bow tuning and limb matching, but as time went on I started to write more about shooting form. Gradually, I became more organized. After all, I'm a teacher, and every Friday I plan all my lessons for the next week.

Good plans avoid problems and confusion; good plans get you more efficiently to your goal.

PRACTICE STRUCTURE
A good practice uses your conscious mind and has the following parts:
1) A warm-up / stretching period;
2) a blank bale / no sight / no target period;
3) a scoring round;
4) bow tuning as needed;
5) a practice-ending blank bale session;
6) stretching / cool down.
This is the way to build meaningful, effective practice sessions.
Let's look at each of these ingredients to see how many arrows need to be shot, what scoring needs to be done, and the record keeping needed to hold it together and keep you moving in the right direction.

Practice Step / Part 1: WARM UP

Starting cold is a physical enemy. Starting time is the most likely time you'll injure yourself, because your muscles aren't ready to work at their highest efficiency. So always warm up. This means warming your muscles before your first arrow in practice and at tournaments. To shoot your best at tournaments, you must practice at your best.

I like to take a short walk before practice, during which I swing my walking stick. I start slowly and gently by swinging the stick back and forth with increasing range and speed. Ten or 15 minutes is enough for me to get loose.

If I've taken my walk earlier in the day, just before shooting I warm up with a rubber exercise band or spring-exerciser. These devices generally are available in sporting goods stores and medical supply stores that handle this type of exercise equipment.

Be sure you use the stretch band correctly. There are many articles already in print on the use of the stretch band to prepare for practice and tournaments. The real work is in developing the discipline to do it regularly.

Practice Step / Part 2:
BLANK BALE PRACTICE ... WITH A PLAN
HAVING FOCUS AND SINGLE-MINDEDNESS

This is where real archers are made -- in front of the bale with a plan, but with no target, no sight. Making the plan is your biggest job for each practice session. Without the plan of form-steps to work on, blank bale shooting will help endurance conditioning only.

To ensure good focus --

1) Remove the target face from the bale so it is as blank as possible.

2) Remove the sight from your bow, or at least take off the sight pin or scope. Then tape over the peep so you can't aim. Aiming draws your conscious mind off the form-step and onto the target.

3) Stand close to the target butt. It works better that way, especially if you're blindfolded. You don't need walking practice, so stand close -- three or four yards -- and you can practice anywhere you can set up a target butt. You can become a better archer by practicing in a closet, if that's all the space you have.

You must focus on the process, not the outcome at the target.

I do these preparations with my shooting school classes and start them shooting. Five minutes later I look at the target butt. I know what I'll see -- most of them have groups of arrows stuck together in the bale.

I stop them and ask what they are doing to get groups. Their answer? "Aiming the second arrow at the first one."

Don't aim, I tell them, so you can focus on the step you want to improve. Close your eyes or wear a blindfold, but do not aim. Focus your conscious-thinking mind on whatever form-step you're working on. Make that form-step your only conscious thought.

The plan must be geared toward form improvement. Beginning, middle and end phases of your plan must **focus on a single form-step that needs attention**. That's right, <u>**one form-step at a time.**</u> When you get one step in shape, only then move to the next.

Where best to start? I recommend **starting with your weakest form-step closest to the beginning of the shot sequence.** A chain is only as strong as its weakest link. That statement may be a cliche`, but it is absolutely true.

In Core Archery, you know that 'stance' is the first step. If your stance is fine, then move to Step Two -- hand position -- and begin working on that, if it needs it, to make it right, relaxed and natural. If Step Two is allright, go to Step Three, and so on through the steps.

In this manner, you work on a building block concept, right from the first level of the foundation.

To bring your conscious mind fully to bear on your bow hand position, for example, you must consciously focus only and totally on hand position throughout the shot process. Let nothing interfere.

Continuing with this example ... make sure you set your hand properly at its first touch to the grip. You must establish and consciously focus on the feel of your hand on that grip. You are consciously focusing on the feel, so that through time the correct feeling act is transferred into your task-performance mind. This is the way it becomes a retained motor action called a habit!

Much research has been done on the subject of practice. Conclusions point to the fact that, on average, humans need about 20 days to establish a new habit. Therefore, plans to improve a form-step must be at least that long until you know your own best time frame to establish a habit. Like the brain surgeon, we aren't concerned about how long the operation takes, only that it is done right.

Your priority here is quality shots, not a high quantity of shots. You should focus on each arrow and how it feels for the particular form-step on which you are training. For best results, shoot four or five arrows per end and take your time with each arrow. Twenty to 25 arrows are enough if you maintain focus for each of them.

Practice Step / Part 3: THE SCORING ROUND

Scoring is one measure of our shooting improvement or decline, so we must have a place for it in our practice plan. Another measure, of course, is the opinion of a coach, but most archers don't have one available. In the absence of a coach, keep score.

CHOOSING A ROUND TO USE

Choosing an appropriate round to use is not difficult. Indoor archery offers good standard rounds; I'd recommend using one of them for indoor practice. For instance, 30 arrows at 20 yards at a Vegas face is a really good standard, as is 60 arrows at the NFAA five-spot indoor target.

If you don't have 20 yards at home, as many don't, shoot at 12 to 15 yards and score the target inside-out. That is, the arrow must be completely inside the ten-ring to count as a ten. You could use the Vegas face with the Super-X ring inside the ten-ring and score it as a ten. Then when you get to shoot at 20 yards, score the regulation ten-ring. Your scores should match closely.

For outdoor scoring, create your own round. For instance, I like shooting 30 arrows at 50 yards using the NFAA hunter target with a 10-centimeter white spot. I also like shooting 36 arrows at 70 meters using the 122-centimeter FITA target.

If you aren't ready for those standards, shooting 30 arrows at 40 yards at an 80-centimeter FITA target may be more appropriate. Or just make a five-inch spot and put it at a comfortable distance.

Whatever the round, keep records of the scores you shoot. When you shoot perfect scores on that round, change the round a little by moving further away or making a smaller spot. Target size and distance are not important as long as you use the same format over a period of time. Using the same round and keeping scoring records are most important.

Over a season of practice, I like looking over my records to see scores, arrows used, bow used and tuning changes made. Checking old notes can help find that little ingredient that gets me back to the top again. It can work the same for you.

A score doesn't need to be shot every practice session. Two or three scores a week are sufficient to monitor progress. Some nights in my basement, I'll just shoot for rhythm and not keep score; but when I go to my local club I always shoot a serious scoring round. I imagine that I'm at a big tournament. This gives me practice shooting in a highly "meaningful" situation.

When you practice at home, you can play around with your set-up and form. Then you can be all business at your local club once or twice a week, or on Sunday and Wednesday night at home.

The main thing is to establish a routine and make certain that you are shooting a serious competitive round sometime during the week. This will let you chart your progress and work on Mental Function 3.

Practice Step / Part 4: BOW TUNING

Do your bow tuning on the days you don't shoot a score. Because bow tuning can take lots of time and lots of arrows, you may need to allocate certain practice days as bow tuning days. If that's not good for you, tune a little before or after you score.

Whatever you do, **don't shoot too many arrows. Practicing when you're tired may reinforce the bad habits that develop when your muscles become fatigued.**

Be sure to log the number of arrows you shoot and the changes you make to your equipment. Sixty arrows per practice session for practice during the indoor season are plenty, but as a tournament gets close you should raise that to 90 per practice session. Outdoors, I shoot more arrows, at least 150 per session, nearing a tournament.

Writing it all down in a logbook, as I mentioned earlier, will help you regulate your total arrows. This helps avoid overshooting and saves time.

In the off-season, you can tune a little during each practice. Without the pressure of a tournament coming soon, you can make one change, shoot your scoring round and make notes about how everything worked, then make another change at the next practice session, and so on. Slowly you will get your set-up working without the big rush you encounter before a tournament.

Practice Step / Part 5:
END-OF–PRACTICE BLANK BALE SHOOTING

Every practice session should end as it began by shooting at a blank bale. You start each session working on a certain form step; when ending that session, reinforce that same step. As before, no target face or sight should be used during this practice phase so the desired feel of the new skill being learned gradually can be passed over to the task-performing mind. Total conscious focus needs to be placed on that one form-step again. Ten or 15 shots are sufficient if you practice with total discipline. Practice properly and expect positive results.

Mindlessly shooting arrows at a blank bale does nothing to improve a person's form; intense conscious thinking about how the form feels does improve it. Only by fully engaging your conscious-thinking mind in the learning process can you hope to transfer form to your task-performing mind. Then, after approximately 20 days of practice on that form-step, your task-performing mind should have retained and be running, for example, your bow hand placement. Your bow hand should naturally, consistently and automatically find its place on the grip area of your bow without conscious guidance. Your conscious mind will then be free to attack another form-step.

Practice Step / Part 6: COOL DOWN

When you have finished shooting arrows, stretch your warm muscles before quitting. This can be done with stretch bands or with isometric stretches. A short walk or run is good, too, if you're also building stamina.

I like to draw my bow with my left hand when I'm done shooting. (I shoot right handed.) I draw 10 to 20 times to stimulate my opposing muscle groups to help prevent stress on my spine and also keep all my muscles in tone.

Developing muscles on both sides of the body and getting good chiropractic care helps eliminate physical problems, increases strength and improves stability no matter what your age.

RECORD KEEPING

I've already said that record keeping is the glue that holds all this hard work together. Good records, when used, help us avoid wasting time relearning a lesson we learned six months ago. We can't humanly remember everything, so we need to record at least the important stuff.

When keeping a log, simpler is better. Here's a form I've developed for my Core Archery shooting schools. Feel free to use it and make changes to suit your own needs. I've filled in one copy so you can see how I use it to keep track of my important practice work.

SHOOTING LOG

DATE_____

OBJECTIVE _____

BOW SET-UP _____

DISTANCE	# SHOTS	NOTES / SCORE	BOW TUNING

LOG SHEET

BB = Blank Bale

SHOOTING LOG

DATE _11/17/03_
OBJECTIVE _MAINTAIN LOW BOW SHOULDER_
BOW SETUP _SUPER NOVA / OMEGA CAM_

DISTANCE	#SHOTS	NOTES/SCORE	BOW TUNING
BB	15	SHOULDER IS WEAK ↑ RIDES UP	—
20 yds	30	296/300 VEGAS FACE	SHORTEN STRING 4 TWISTS
20 yds	10	—	SHORTEN 4 MORE TWISTS
BB	6	SHOULDER VERY WEAK	—

STEP-BY-STEP LEARNING

Our objective for practice is to transfer the control of each form-step from our conscious mind to our task-performing mind. Our conscious mind controls the action while we are learning the skill. Time-on-task, approximately 20 days of it, will establish the neural links and the motor conditioning needed to retain the skill.

Once one form-step is learned, we move to the next form-step in the shot sequence. If, for 20 practices, you worked on Step 3 (hand position), then move on to Step 4 (setting your posture). If you already have that in shape, go to the next step in your sequence. Do this until you have learned and retained every form-step.

CONSCIOUS THINKING - 20 PRACTICES - TASK RETENTION

As you can see, form building may take a while. There is no shortcut approach. Commit to a work schedule over six months and build your own model form.

You will get the results you want only by working hard and smart. The hard part is doing the practice. The smart part is keeping the shooting log and using your conscious mind to learn each form-step in its turn.

START NOW

Why wait for the next tournament to be completed before starting on your form-step improvement? If you are not presently satisfied with your shooting, then at least repair one form-step now. You can get started on that first corrective measure and work on it through the next tournament.

If you elect to start now, don't expect to shoot your highest score at the next tournament. Remember, while you are shooting each and every tournament arrow, you'll consciously be focusing on a single form-step, and that means you won't be operating your competitive mental plan. Starting now means you are more interested in the long-range goal of improved form than you are in winning this tournament. Increasing the number of shots you execute with improved form will be your goal for this tournament.

PRACTICE NEVER ENDS

You'll be able to use your practice log and blank bale skills to revise, repair and rebuild any step that develops a little flaw, but how will you know when there is a flaw?

There are at least three methods you can use:
1) A coach who sees you shoot periodically;
2) videotape,
3) your score trend.

When your scores are going down and you can't figure out why, you need a coach or videotape. My friend, Bill, sees me shoot every now and then. He sees me just often enough to notice any changes in my body position, head position or follow-through. He tells me what he sees, and then it's up to me to make the corrections. If you have someone like this to check your form, you already know what a great advantage it is.

If you have no one to act as an extra pair of eyes, use a video camera. Tape yourself shooting every month or every other month. Compare your present self to your former self and note any differences. If you see some significant flaw, begin taking corrective action. Don't wait! Keep on top of your form all the time – form first, then the score.

CONCLUSION

Using the powers of your conscious mind, you can teach your body to execute correct form. Through time and practice, you can transfer control of that physical form to your task-performing mind that can run hundreds of operations at the same time. Therefore, the physical part of shooting becomes mindless as far as the conscious is concerned. It happens naturally, without us consciously controlling any step.

Driving your car is like this. We learn to drive over several years, and it becomes an act we don't consciously think about. (In education, we call this a "non-cognitive" activity.) So, during a short drive to town, we consciously think about many things unrelated to driving ... and before we know it we're three blocks past the store where we wanted to stop. We didn't hit anything with our car; we made the right turns, and we stopped at all the stop signs. We made it safely because our task-performing mind was doing all that for us.

Shooting an arrow must become a habit like driving your car.

Mental Function 3
HIGH PERFORMANCE
Embedding your conscious mind <u>WITHIN</u> your shooting form

THE HAILSTORM
What happens when you're driving along and it begins to rain, snow or even hail? What do you do first? I turn off the radio first because it distracts me from driving, and I tell everyone in the car to be quiet so I can concentrate!

Why do they distract me now when only moments before they didn't? It distracts me now because driving has become a conscious control or cognitive activity. My conscious monitor has detected a nonstandard situation, causing my conscious mind to be engaged in my driving. I must now take in as much information as possible about the conditions, so I'll be ready if I have to make any quick conscious decisions.

When the hailstorm starts, how do you drive? White knuckled? You have to keep the car on the road and get where you're going safely. You tighten up mentally, and by the time you get through the storm you're tight physically. Smooth and relaxed performance is no longer possible. Once you're through the storm, you are exhausted. You're so tight it takes you hours to relax.

During the hailstorm, you are fully engaged in conscious thought about your driving, and this is exactly where many archers are when they get to a tournament – they are in the middle of a hailstorm! They try to focus their conscious mind on every detail, and their mental tightness makes them physically tight. Since they have not practiced that way (physically tight), they shoot poorly.

You don't practice shooting white knuckled, so you can't afford to shoot that way in a tournament. How to avoid it, when you and I both know we're going to be nervous at the start of a tournament round? How do we keep from tightening up mentally? How do some guys do it and some don't? What's the secret?

The secret is there is no secret; there's a plan. Some lucky athletes are born with a built-in mental plan, but most of us have to develop one. Yes, develop a competitive mental plan just like we develop a physical-form plan. You can, and you must, develop a competitive mental plan if you want to reach your full potential.

Let's examine the Twelve Steps of Core Archery and my conscious links to them.

A SAMPLE MENTAL PLAN

FORM STEPS	CONSCIOUS THOUGHT
1) Stance --------------->	1) Image the Arrow Striking the Target Middle
2) Nock	
3) Hand Position	
4) Posture -------------->	2) Breathe / Relax and Visually Acquire Target
5) Raise	
6) Draw	
7) Full Draw ----------->	3) Set Shoulder & Rhomboids
8) Aim / Tighten	
9) Aim ----------------->	4) Aim
10) Release	
11) Follow Through --->	5) Evaluate
12) Reset --------------->	6) Breathe / Relax

This is my plan. I run it during every shot when I am tournament-ready. The closer I get to a tournament, the more I must practice running my mental game plan until it becomes fully embedded in my shooting routine. Thinking these thoughts, I've determined, contributes to my ability to make the shot.

You may find other thoughts that work better for you. You also may find that a different sequence is better for you. Experiment until you get the plan that works best for you.

However, before examining the conscious thought steps, let's first look at the overall situation with your conscious mind, to set the scene, so to speak.

YOUR CONSCIOUS MIND AS YOUR POSITIVE PARTNER

If your task-performing mind is running your form, what is your conscious mind doing? This is the most serious question most people will face in archery. The thoughts **you are allowing** to occur in your conscious mind during your shooting are of the greatest importance for your scoring success.

Recall the premise with which I began this chapter:

PREMISE: **To reach your full archery potential you must bring your conscious mind fully to bear <u>ON</u> and then <u>WITHIN</u> the act of shooting.**

We use our conscious mind to work "on" our form in practice, but when we shoot tournament archery we have to develop a plan to use our conscious mind "within" our form.

You need to make your conscious mind your positive partner if you want positive results. If you allow your conscious mind to remain outside the shooting process, it is an outside controller, and it inevitably will think outside thoughts that distract your task-performing mind from your goal. **A wandering conscious mind is most athletes' downfall.** You must train your conscious mind to stay on task so it doesn't wander off during a serious scoring round.

This can be done. You <u>can</u> train your conscious mind to be your positive partner in the shooting act. You must bring it "within" the shooting act, through training, so that any conscious thoughts you have will influence your form in a positive but non-controlling way. You must train it to think within your form. You trained your body to shoot with a desired physical form, and now you must train your conscious mind to fit inside that form as a positive partner.

This is why my first mental game plan of "shoot your form" was on the right track. It wasn't the best plan, but it kept me focused on form most of the time. It kept my conscious mind from trying to micro-manage each form-step, and I was able to shoot in a fluid manner.

One thing you can't do, I believe, is to prevent your conscious mind from having thoughts. It always is thinking, so you must accept that it always is thinking and use those thoughts to your advantage. This is how you get to the "zone" athletes talk about, or where, as the Zen masters say, "body and mind become one".

THE CONSCIOUS MENTAL PLAN

A plan leads to a higher success rate. The right plan will embed your conscious thinking within your form-steps -- thinking that is positive and cooperative with your shooting sequence. This thinking creates the best conditions for shooting success.

The Core Archery Mental Plan for tournament shooting links specific conscious thoughts to key form steps. The thoughts have to be specific so you can discipline your conscious to them -- thoughts you can rely on to keep you in familiar territory while your task-performing mind is executing your form. Shot after shot, you must think the same thought at the same time in your form-steps.

This plan, then, depends on you having your form-steps committed to your task-performance mind. With that done, you build conscious links into those steps, links that are meaningful to you and that you can easily train yourself to do over and over.

You should be able to write these in sequence beside your 12 physical steps. If you write them down, you can practice and revise them until you think them on every shot. You practice them until they are embedded within your form instead of outside it.

Now let's look at the **CONSCIOUS THOUGHT steps** of my plan. This is my explanation for each part.

Step 1: THE IMAGE

You have read or heard about the powers of mental imagery. Believe me when I say that most of it's true. There is real power in creating a mental image of something happening and then setting out physically to make it happen.

Somewhere near the very beginning of your form-steps, you must create the mental image of your arrow going into the center of the target. You must see it as real in your mind. Your body won't know the difference between thinking it and the actual event, so imagine it to prepare your body for the real event.

As I make the final settling into my stance and reach for an arrow, I begin an image event -- I see myself, making it a type of out-of-body experience -- that vividly displays me aiming intensely at the center of the target, and then the arrow flying perfectly to the "x". From my earliest days in archery, I have loved to watch arrow flight. It's a thing of beauty. So I use that image here as a calming feeling and to help create an expected result.

At this point, when I'm shooting well, I am lost to the real world and totally in tune with the shot sequence. The outside world becomes very small and fades away; I am focused. As the outside world shrinks away, the target grows larger until that is all there is in my world. When I see the target so big, I know the arrow will hit it.

When there's interference, I can't get focused in my image. Thoughts of other things past, present or future are still there in some form, and I must recognize that and check-off on the shot. I start over, with a clearer conscious mind.

This is where any archer uses the conscious mind monitor to terminate the shot when some aspect of the routine does not pass for normal or expected.

Step 2: BREATH/RELAX & VISUALLY ACQUIRE TARGET

Somewhere near the time when I check my head and shoulder posture, I visually acquire the center of the target. I'm breathing inward as I raise the bow, staying relaxed. I consciously look at the "x" area on the target so my entire body is now oriented and aiming toward the center. I'm adjusting my whole being to the location of the "x" ring, knowing that the arrow is going to hit it.

By now I am beginning to draw the bow. My inhaling ends and exhaling begins, and the center of the target appears to grow in size.

From this point on, I don't take my eyes off the target center until the arrow has entered the target. Staying visually locked on the target is essential for consistency.

You must position your body the same in relation to the target for every shot and throughout the shot, and this visual locking-on is part of it. You read this in an earlier chapter, but it needs reinforcing here.

Step 3: SET RHOMBOIDS FOR BACK TENSION

Setting my rhomboids for back tension is my shooting objective. I feel, therefore, it must be part of my mental plan. It is extremely important to have a conscious thought about setting my scapula and engaging my rhomboids to near full power. Without rhomboid action, I won't execute the shot as I practiced, so I must be sure to make that action happen.

Once I'm set, my concious thought rejoins my locked-on eye contact on the center of the target. I find this easy to do because I know the arrow is going to hit the "x" when the shot releases. It's like going home.

Step 4: AIM

By now, I have exhaled two-thirds of my breath. My full-draw position has been established, and my bow sight has entered into my vision. I am now aiming my body and sighting the bow. My conscious mind also must move to aiming. Nothing else can be in my mind. I am totally -- physically and mentally -- involved in aiming.

This is "zone" status here because the mind is in unison with the body; it is within the shooting form, contributing positively to the shot.

Any interrupting thought now is cause for aborting the shot. A breakdown still may happen, especially when you are in a meaningful situation, whether in practice or a tournament. Your conscious mind monitor may sense that something is nonstandard with your aiming. When the alarm goes off in your conscious mind, you must heed the call. After all, your body and mind must combine for a successful joint venture. If they do not, success is in jeopardy.

Training brings about the monitor and the alarm system. Let down, breath to relax, let any interrupting thoughts pass and start over with the image of the arrow hitting the "x".

STEP 5: EVALUATE & SEPARATE

This has to be a short step. You don't have time to dwell on it, but do take a second -- but only a second -- to evaluate the shot.

One of four things has happened:
1) You shot it well and it hit the center.
2) You shot it well and it missed the center.
3) You shot it poorly and it hit the center.
4) You shot it poorly and it missed the center.

Accept the result. You can't change it, so don't let it change you. Do one of these appropriate actions:
- Reward yourself if it was a #1.
- Check your equipment if it was a #2.
- Give thanks if it was a #3.
- Be determined to execute better if #4.

Keep it simple here, and don't beat yourself up over it. It's only one archery shot, not life. You are still a good person if you missed the 'x'. The worst thing to happen is that you earn a slightly lesser score than you could have had. Remember, you'll do better on the next shot.

Now you have to take the big step -- separate from the shot. Don't go forward with it strapped to your back or in your mind. If you do, it will get very, very heavy, especially if you try to carry several other shots with it. It will get so heavy you will soon be shooting from your knees. Shooting is much more difficult when your chin is on your chest and your lower lip is dragging on the floor. Believe me, it's hard to aim when you're stepping on your lip.

Forget the shot entirely. Go to the next shot free of any mental baggage from a less-than-perfect shot. Stuff happens.

Also – and this is an important also -- go to the next shot free of excess euphoria brought on by a perfect shot. Just move on to the next shot ready to conduct business as usual. In computer jargon, perform a "Ctrl-Alt + Del"!

PRACTICE YOUR PLAN

Using this sample you can build your own mental plan. It should have several important ingredients – a mental image step, a thought about your shooting objective, and conscious aiming.

Plan Your Work, Then Work Your Plan

Practicing your mental steps during simulated tournament rounds at home or at your local club is vital to your success. As I mentioned earlier, when I go to my local club I always shoot a serious score. I pretend I'm at the next tournament I plan to attend.

I make it very businesslike, so I become accustomed to being totally focused for an official round. I use the official target, the prescribed number of practice arrows and, indoors, I switch target positions from top-to-bottom or bottom-to-top at the halfway point of the round. I also picture the setting, block out the noises and wait the prescribed time between ends. By making it real, I make myself ready for the tournament.

CONCLUSION: TRUST IN YOUR FORM, WORK SMART

To reach your potential in archery, you must use all your mental abilities. You use them first to develop your form and then to compliment that form during tournaments. You need your strongest mental plan to reach your full potential.

What about the others who have a plan just as good as yours? What about those who have a great plan and great physical skills to go with it? How can you beat them?

The answer is simple -- trust. The degree of trust in your plan is the determining factor as to who wins. If you invest your energy and talent into building a form and a mental plan, then you should have all the confidence in the world that it will work. You trust it in practice, so you must trust it in tournaments.

To build that trust, you must work smart. I know that what you have learned in this book can help you do that. Work smart to build and execute your Core Archery Plan, and you will get to a higher performance level.

Shoot straight; keep well.

In 1999 I listened for the first time to Olympic Champion Lanny Basham's audio tapes on "Mental Management". His ideas confirmed many of the habits I had already established. The way he organized his own training, scheduled practice and kept notes prompted me to do more with my own program and what I teach at my shooting schools. What you learn from Lanny is that to be your best, you must get organized.

The AUTHOR -- LARRY WISE

EDUCATION
1965 graduate of Juniata Joint High School, Pennsylvania
1969 graduate of Lycoming College, BA (mathematics)
1977 graduate of Pennsylvania State University, Master of Education

OCCUPATION
1) Public school educator of Algebra, geometry, trigonometry , calculus and advanced calculus. Employed by the Juniata County School District 1969-2004.
2) Professional archer since 1978
3) Author (books, magazine articles and columns) since 1985
4) Video writer, director and performer since 1987

PROFESSIONAL MEMBERSHIPS
1) Pennsylvania State Education Association
2) National Field Archery Association
3) National Archery Association

PROFESSIONAL ARCHERY POSITIONS
1) NFAA Pro Division Chairman, 1983-85
2) PAA Vice President, 1987-88
3) Jennings Compound Bow Staff, 1979-82
4) Bear Archery Staff. 1983-88
5) Golden Key Futura Staff, 1986-91
6) Indian Ind./Xi Bows Tournament Staff, Director & Design Consultant, 1989-97
7) Golden Eagle Archery, 1997-99
8) Merlin Bows of England, 2000-present

AMATEUR TOURNAMENT RECORD
1978 Pennsylvania State Indoor champion	1978 Atlantic City Classic champion
1978 North American Indoor champion	1978 NFAA National Field 2nd place

PROFESSIONAL TOURNAMENT RECORD
1978 Lake of the Woods, 2nd place in 1st flight	1986 Big Sky Team Champion with Ron Walker
1979 World Team Champion with Jack Cramer	1986 NFAA-EASTON Pro Points Champion
1980 World Team Champion with Jack Cramer	1986 IFAA World Champion, Blair Atholl, Scotland
1981 Big Sky Team Champion	1987 PA State Indoor, 1st
1981 World Team Champion with Jack Cramer	1987 PAA National Team Champion with Ron Walker
1982 Atlantic City Classic, 1st place	1987 Coors Silver Dollar Open, 1st (600 perfect)
1982 Atlantic City Classic FITA I and FITA II, 1st	1988 New England Open, 1st (600 perfect score)
1982 NFAA Indoor Sectional, 1st	1988 NFAA Indoor Champion with Dean Pridgen
1982 Las Vegas Team Champion	1988 NFAA Field Pro-Am, 1st with Bob Davis
1982 Las Vegas, 2nd place to Dean Pridgen after record 23 arrow, sudden-death shoot-off	1988 PA State Target Champion
1982 NFAA National Field, 2nd place	1988 PAA Points Ranking, 2nd
1983 Big Sky Open, 1st place	1989 Nelson's Indoor, 1st (599/600)
1983 NFAA National Field, 2nd place	1990 Minn. Open Indoor, 1st (59x/60x)
1983 NFAA Pro Points Champion	1990 New England Open, 1st (599/600)
1984 Long Island Open, 1st (900 perfect score)	1990 Big Sky Open, 2nd place
1984 Milwaukee Sentinel Sports Show, 1st (750 perfect score)	1990 NFAA Field Pro-Am, 1st
1984 NFAA Pro Points, 2nd place	1990 PAA Points Ranking, 2nd
1985 Mike's Pro-Am, 1st (450 perfect score)	1991 PA State Indoor, 1st
1985 L & K Open, 2nd (900 perfect score)	1991 NFAA Indoor Sectional, 1st
1985 Maid of the Mist Open, 1st (551 + 554)	1991 PAA Outdoor, 3rd
1985 World Team Champion with Ron Walker	1991 NFAA Field Pro Team, 2nd
1985 NFAA Pro Points, 4th	1991 10,000 Lakes Open, 1st (592/600 at 50 yds.)
1986 Mike's Pro-Am, 1st (450 perfect score)	1991 PAA Points Ranking, 6th
1986 Las Vegas, 1st place tie (899/900, 2nd place)	1992 PAA Outdoor 4th
1986 New England Open, 1st (600 perfect score)	1992 BIG SKY 3 rd
1986 PA State Indoor, 1st	1993 Las Vegas Open 1st place tie, 4th place
1986 Ann Marston Open, 1st (900 perfect score)	1993 Atlantic City, 4th place
	1993 PAA Outdoor, 4th place
	1994 IFAA World Field, England, 2nd Place

1995	Las Vegas, 9th Place	1997	New Zealand and Australia Shooters' School Coach
1995	PA State Indoor record of 1199/1200 including first ever 20-yard perfect 600 at PA Championships	1997	NFAA Outdoor nationals, 10th place
1996	NFAA Outdoor Nationals 5th place	1998	NFAA Master Coach School Instructor
1996	IFAA World Championship 4th place	1998	Keshet Eilon, Israel, Archery Coach
1997	NAA Level 3 Coaches Course	2000	NAA Level 4 Coaches Course

BOWHUNTING

Since 1976, when I began bowhunting with a compound, I have taken 30 whitetail deer in Pennsylvania, New York and Michigan. I also tagged a wild pig in New Zealand in 1997.

SEMINARS

In 1979, in cooperation with Sherwood Schoch Associates, I began conducting seminars on tuning the compound bow. Since that time, I have conducted more than 300 such seminars and shooting demonstrations in 20 states.

BOOKS

Target Communications
1985   TUNING YOUR COMPOUND BOW
1989   TUNING & SILENCING YOUR BOWHUNTING SYSTEM
1994   TUNING & SHOOTING YOUR 3-D BOW
2004   CORE ARCHERY

Stackpole Books
1992   BOW AND ARROW: A COMPREHENSIVE GUIDE TO
EQUIPMENT, TECHNIQUE AND TOURNAMENTS.

VIDEO TAPES

In 1987, I completed a video tape with Bear Archery on tuning the compound bow. I provided technical inserts for the Quest Videos "Tune Up For Bucks" video in 1992 and in November of 1993 I completed three videos for Robin Hood Productions. These latest three films are geared for 3-D archers and their equipment. In June, 1995, my son, wife and I helped Robin Hood Videos produce " A Guide To Beginning Archery" which was released in September, 1995. The Master Coaches Series by Robin Hood Videos was released in January, 1999.

BOW DESIGN

I joined Indian Industries in 1989, and helped the engineering staff develop the Premiere, Larry Wise Signature tournament bow and helped on several other bow and arrow rest projects. I have designed several bows for Golden Eagle Archery that were released in late 1999. I helped design the Merlin Super Nova handle in 2002 to achieve the best grip-area design to allow proper hand placement.

COACHING

Since 1996, I have been involved in NAA coaching at the Olympic Training Centers in Lake Placid, NY, and San Diego, CA. In August, 1997, after earning Level Three coaching certification, I was selected to be a member of the 20-coach developmental coaching staff for NAA and have been participating in the restructuring of the student and coaching manuals.

I spent nine days coaching compound archers in New Zealand and Australia during 1997.

Every summer from 1998 thru 2001 I travel to Israel to coach at the Keshet Eilon Master Violin Course where young violinists from 20 countries receive instruction from violin great Schlomo Mintz, among others. They also learn archery every day to enhance their playing form.

I also conduct one- and two-day shooting schools at archery dealerships along the East Coast of the U.S.

CONTACT
* 1-877-Go4-XXXs (464-9997)   (toll free)
* www.larrywise.com

*The PUBLISHER

This is the fourth book written by Larry Wise that Target Communications has published.

The company has published 16 titles in an "On Target" series on archery, bowhunting, deer hunting, muzzleloader shooting and wild game cooking.

Glenn Helgeland, president of Target Communications, has been a magazine and book editor and publisher since 1968. He was editor/associate publisher of *ARCHERY WORLD* (now *BOWHUNTING WORLD*) magazine and won awards from the National Archery Association for service to archery and from the National Shooting Sports Foundation for a series of articles titled "The Hunter's Story".

He was the founding editor and associate publisher of *ARCHERY RETAILER* (now *ARCHERY BUSINESS*) magazine.

He has been, at various times, bowhunting columnist for *FINS & FEATHERS*, *AMERICAN HUNTER*, *NORTH AMERICAN HUNTER* and *BOWHUNTING WORLD*, and a marketing and sales promotion columnist for *ARCHERY BUSINESS*.

Helgeland co-authored, with John Williams, men's 1972 Olympic archery gold medalist, the book "Archery For Beginners". He also edited the 2nd edition of the Pope and Young Club's Big Game Records Book.

Before becoming involved in archery/bowhunting writing and publishing, Helgeland was associate editor of *NATIONAL WILDLIFE* magazine.

He is a member and past director of National Association of Consumer Shows (NACS) and a member of Professional Outdoor Communicators Association (POMA).